WINNING
Single Wing Football

7/6/05

Best wishes to

Roger West —

Sincerely,
Ken Keuffel

To My Best Coach   10/7/06
Cheers
Kirk Cordardy

WINNING
Single Wing Football

A Simplified Guide
for the Football Coach

Kenneth W. Keuffel, Ph.D.

Swift Press
Lawrenceville, New Jersey

Although the author and publisher have made every effort to ensure the accuracy and completeness of information contained in this book, we assume no responsibility for errors, inaccuracies, omissions, or any inconsistency herein. Any slights of people, places, or organizations are unintentional.

First printing 2004

ISBN 0-9744022-4-9
LCCN 2003095782

ATTENTION CORPORATIONS, UNIVERSITIES, COLLEGES, AND PROFESSIONAL ORGANIZATIONS: Quantity discounts are available on bulk purchases of this book for educational, gift purposes, or as premiums for increasing magazine subscriptions or renewals. Special books or book excerpts can also be created to fit specific needs. For information, please contact Swift Press, 2711 Main Street, Lawrenceville, NJ 08648-1014; (609) 896-1813; www.singlewingfootball.com.

To Betsy,
my devoted wife,
for every reason.

Acknowledgments

My friends Steve Van Savage and Ed Racely were kind enough to read my typed manuscript and offer suggestions. To them, many thanks.

I am most grateful to Elsie Van Savage, who was the off-site repository of countless manuscript and diagram files. Thank you, Elsie, for this help.

I am indebted to Wabash College for permission to use a picture of a skeleton backfield. That was most helpful.

Above all, I owe my greatest debt of gratitude to my wife for her never-failing encouragement and assistance.

Table of Contents

Foreword

Ken Keuffel was a giant among giants. He was a contemporary of the great single wing coaches who dominated the game for so many years. Names like Charlie Caldwell and Dick Colman of Princeton, George Munger of Penn, Fritz Crisler of Michigan, John Stiegman of Rutgers and Penn, Bowden Wyatt of Tennessee, Bernie Bierman of Minnesota, Lou Little of Columbia, Carl Snavely of Cornell and North Carolina, et al. All were names synonymous with the single wing era of college football.

By writing this book Ken presents not only his unique style of play that was developed over the years but also many of the thoughts and philosophies of these "Masters." His intention in presenting this book as a guide for coaching the single wing offense has evolved into much more. It is not only a well-written, concise book in which all aspects of the single wing are presented, but it is also a presentation of a successful coaching philosophy that has been cultivated over a long career.

Coaching football is much more than formations and diagrams. It is a complex game that requires detailed planning, organization, and preparation. Players must play to the best of their ability; they must be disciplined and willing to meet the demands of both the practice field and the day of the game. These are the requisites of success in football, as they are in life, and are the hallmark of Coach Keuffel's coaching philosophy.

In addition, the chapter on the quick kick as an offensive weapon is an absolute "must read" chapter for every coach at every level of the game. Its place in Ken's offensive scheme is indeed compelling.

Ken Keuffel has been head coach of single wing football teams for 37 years. For 31 of these seasons he coached at Lawrenceville School, where his win-loss record was a stellar 159-89-8. In the early 1960s Ken was the head football coach at Wabash College, where his six-year record was 28-20-5. Without question, while coaching the single wing, he has compiled a most successful record.

I wholeheartedly recommend *Winning Single Wing Football* to coaches in particular, but also to the many players and students of football who want to gain as much knowledge and understanding of this great American game as possible.

—*Harry T. Gamble*

Editor's note: *Harry Gamble has had a distinguished and unique career in football, ranging from being a high school coach for 8 years to being president of the Philadelphia Eagles for 10 years. Along the way he has been an assistant college coach, an assistant coach for the Eagles, a college head coach for 14 years at Lafayette and Penn, and coordinator of football operations for the National Football League.*

In his "retirement" Harry goes abroad each summer to coach Russian high school kids in American football under the auspices of the National Football League.—June 2003

Preface

In my 37 years as a head coach, our unbalanced line single wing offense has been successful in both schoolboy and college coaching. At Lawrenceville School our 31-year record was 159-89-8. Along the way we enjoyed four undefeated seasons, and five seasons with only one loss. Against our big traditional rival we had 23 wins and only 8 losses.

Playing mainly larger colleges, the Wabash College Little Giants achieved a six-year record of 28-20-5. Our 1965 Wabash team was twelfth among all colleges in the country in average yards gained rushing a game.

Offense is only part of the game. I would never minimize the importance of defense, the kicking game, and various intangible factors in coaching winning football, but I am convinced that much of whatever success we have had is due to our single wing offense.

In 1964, when I was coaching at Wabash College, I wrote a book titled *Simplified Single Wing Football*, published by Prentice-Hall, which is out of print. The many inquiries about that book have convinced me that another discussion of our offense is warranted. In the following pages I cover much new ground, ground with which I was unfamiliar in 1964, when I wrote my earlier book.

Now that I am retired, I want to pass along any information about my offense that may be helpful to other coaches. In the upcoming pages I will discuss only those plays and maneuvers we ourselves have coached and used. There is nothing here that is theoretical: Everything has been mastered and applied successfully by schoolboy and small-college players over many years of coaching.

What This Book Covers

In the first chapter I discuss my evolution as a football coach and mention the many factors that influenced me in my choosing this profession. As a player and young coach I was fortunate to be associated with a number of masters of the single wing. Some of these coaches were inducted into the College Hall of Fame, and some were honored by being elected National College Coach of the Year. In addition to these outstanding mentors, I learned from many other coaches whose ideas influenced my thinking.

Next there are chapters on setting up a single wing offense and on teaching individual position play. I covered some of the material in these two chapters in my earlier book. Many of the basic concepts and techniques of the offense remain the same. The following four chapters are completely new as I discuss in detail my current single wing offense: straight series running plays, indirect attack plays, the passing game, and the quick-kicking game.

The discussion of the passing game, in particular, is much more comprehensive than that of my previous book, suggesting how extensive this phase of our offense has become. Even at the high school level, the single wing can be a productive passing offense: In the last seven games of the 1972 Lawrenceville School season, we completed 20 touchdown passes.

Chapter 8 (The Use of Variations) is required reading for the single wing coach. In  this discussion I show how to use variations of the basic formation to keep the defense off balance. Unless a coach has much better players than the opposition, he will need to know how to use variations.

In Chapter 9 (Preparing for a Season) I cover the planning and activities that would face a typical high school single wing coach from the end of one season to the beginning of the next season. Included here are topics such as planning to get maximum benefit from movies, compiling an offense notebook, deciding what to teach first, making practices productive, and setting up a game plan.

In Chapter 10 I discuss helpful aspects of single wing strategy. Here I include topics such as attacking obvious defensive weaknesses, setting up categories of plays, aligning players to advantage, and using false key plays.

Finally, there is a chapter on the values of football and the role of the high school coach as master teacher. These are subjects about which I feel strongly. My remarks in this chapter are not limited to those using the single wing but apply to all the boys who play this great game and the men who coach them.

Single Wing Is Not Difficult to Teach

There is a prevalent myth that it is extremely difficult to introduce and teach the single wing offense. As with any style of attack, it can be difficult to put in this formation if you go about it the wrong way. But if you keep in mind a few simple steps essential to building this offense, it is not difficult to teach.

I discuss this subject in detail in Chapter 9, but I will say here that the most important thing is to train a couple of dependable centers before you do anything else. Your centers must learn to pass competently before you can run any plays. I have a section on teaching the center in Chapter 3. There are other important steps that I will discuss in detail later on. Finally, make sure you show your squad a film or two of a good single wing team in action before you begin practice. Kids have to see to believe.

In 1961, my first season at Wabash College, we started with an inexperienced squad that had won only one game while losing eight the previous year. In their first year with our offense these young men finished with a record of 5 wins and 4 losses, the first winning season at that college in four years. The success we enjoyed with that squad demonstrated we were teaching a single wing system that could be absorbed quickly by players completely unfamiliar with the formation.

An equally compelling example of the feasibility of teaching this offense came in 1992 when I helped Coach Jim Benedict introduce the single wing to his Summit (N.J.) High School team. Looking for something new, Jim came to me for help in the off-season, and by means of discussions and films I was able to school him in this offense well enough that in the first season his team achieved a record of 8 wins and only 3 losses. The next season their record was 11 wins and no losses as they won the state championship.

Before their early practice started, the Summit coaches trained some centers on basic snapping techniques and worked with their tailbacks on different skills. Furthermore, during early practice they followed our advice not to put in too much offense too soon. This is the approach I have advocated when helping other coaches to introduce our offense.

Unfamiliarity Is an Advantage

With so few teams using the single wing today, we have enjoyed a distinct advantage. Time and again opposing coaches have told me it is extremely difficult in one week of practice time to prepare their boys to face an offense they see only once a year.

It is easy to forget how little practice time there is to prepare for a given opponent. Usually during the season you have only three real work days in any week: Tuesday, Wednesday, and Thursday. So you will actually have at most nine or ten hours a week of practice time on the field. If we assume that at least half of this time will be devoted to offense and the kicking game, you will have perhaps four or five hours to spend on the field in defensive preparations for an unfamiliar offense.

And time is not the only problem. You must also train a group of jayvees to simulate an opponent's single wing offense so that your varsity players can work on recognizing and reacting to plays they will encounter in the game. This is a formidable task.

Jordan Olivar, for many years a successful head coach at Yale University, summed up the problem for me. I am grateful to Coach Olivar for writing these pertinent comments in his letter of July 18, 1963:

As far as I am concerned, there is no such thing as simplified single wing football when you are on defense. Boys today come up through three or four years of high school football and one or two years of college ball before they ever see a single wing team from a defensive viewpoint. Then in three days, we expect them to adjust to the new tactics presented to them. It is practically an impossibility. Somehow or other our jayvees on Tuesday and Wednesday never did run the single wing with quite the same efficiency as the varsity got to see it on Saturday afternoon from our opponents.

The timing of the single wing is so different from the T formation that boys continually face, that the defense just gets out of position enough and is unable to react the way they do to the T. The continual double team and trap of the single wing presents an entirely different defensive problem from the T formation. As a result, when we would play a single wing team, such as Princeton, we were always trying to outscore them rather than just trying to hold them. You might also know that when the single wing is applied the way it should be, it is as beautiful to watch as any T formation.

A more dramatic statement came in the opening sentences of an account of one of our victories by George O'Gorman of *The Trentonian*, a Trenton (N.J.) newspaper, on October 11, 1981: *Watching Lawrenceville School's legendary single wing offense at its best is an experience. Trying to defend against it can be a nightmare.*

A Final Word

Quite apart from its unfamiliarity, the unbalanced line single wing is a sound and effective formation. With imaginative planning, simplified teaching techniques, and an insistence on the proper execution of the fundamentals of football, this style of offense can be highly successful.

Above and beyond its intrinsic merits, its novelty can be a determining factor. If the other team is flat-out better than you are, if their players are faster and stronger, you will not expect to win. But if your material is equal or close to equal, the unbalanced line single wing can give you an edge.

There is one other important point to remember about using this offense: Your coaches will like teaching it, and your players will love playing in it. They will enjoy using something different. And they will savor the feeling that their opponents will never really understand what they're doing on offense.

Chapter 1

The EVOLUTION of a FOOTBALL COACH

Like most American boys, I grew up loving football. I knew the name of every college football star. In the thirties radio announcers like Ted Husing and Bill Stern were household names, and we listened to games with great interest. I played in my first high school game at age 15, but the greatest influence on me in my eventual choice to become a football coach was my coach at Phillips Academy (Andover) named Steve Sorota. Steve had played fullback from 1933 to 1935 on nationally ranked Fordham teams under Jim Crowley, one of the Notre Dame Four Horsemen. Steve was a dedicated student of the game. More importantly, he was a superb worker with boys.

Steve's approach was always designed to build a boy's self-confidence. He would constantly encourage a player in his quiet way. Steve was a great teacher. He taught me sound techniques of the fundamentals: blocking, tackling, ball-carrying, passing, pass receiving, punting, and place-kicking. Steve had infinite patience. And patience was something he needed a lot of with a 16-year-old athlete like me. Sixty years later, I can still hear his voice.

Steve encouraged me to run track in the off-season to increase my speed, and he urged me to do manual labor during the summer before my senior year. (In 1941 no football player believed in lifting weights.) All this, I now realize, was part of paying the price.

In my senior year, when I was the captain of the Andover team, early in the preseason I dropped a pass as a result of not being focused. In a rare display of harsh criticism, Steve climbed all over me. He said we had an excellent passer in Bobby Furse, who later set passing records at Yale University, and he wanted to throw the ball more. Playing the Notre Dame Box formation, Bobby was often the tailback, and I was often the wingback. So he would pass to me a lot.

Steve's point in criticizing me vigorously was that we had the makings of an outstanding passing attack, and he wanted to make sure we capitalized on our potential. He knew I was a good receiver; he didn't want me to drop passes. In fact, I didn't drop another pass all season long.

In that 1941 season we ended up with an unbeaten record, and I've never forgotten the feeling of camaraderie and unity that prevailed on that Andover team. It was something I always hoped to replicate with my own teams when I became a coach. The hard work we put in as teammates—and its subsequent reward—was an experience I never forgot. Is it any wonder that, as a coach, I firmly believed in the values we try to teach our young players?

In the late summer of 1942 I enlisted in the Navy and was sent to Chapel Hill Pre-Flight School. Soon I made the Pre-Flight football squad coached by Jim Crowley, Steve Sorota's former coach, who was now a lieutenant commander in the Navy. At Fordham, Coach Crowley had a nine-year record of 56 wins, 13 losses, and 7 ties, one of the best in the country. It was a thrill for an 18-year-old to be coached by him. That season I never played a minute in a regular game, but I could hardly expect to see action on a squad made up of former college and pro players.

I admired Jim Crowley as a person and a coach. He had superb material to work with, but that team played poorly. They were talented individuals who had no identity and barely knew each other's names. There is a lesson here I never forgot: Without unity on a squad, even the best of coaches will have difficulties coaching excellent players.

That team used the familiar balanced line Notre Dame offense but employed some modifications in the backfield shift to take advantage of different personnel. I had no clue as to such subtleties until years later when, as a coach, I studied films of the Fordham teams of the 1938–1941 era. From those films I picked up some helpful ideas, especially the half spin (tailback to fullback) action pass fake I later adjusted to our unbalanced line formation. (See Chapter 6.)

The next main influence that led me to my later becoming a football coach came in a Navy wartime program playing at Princeton University in 1943 under Harry Mahnken. Later Harry became a lifelong friend, and we often talked football. He was a strong believer in a powerful running game and especially in the fact that

you win games with few plays—plays you can only execute to perfection by much repetition.

Some say teaching the fullback full spin is a long and tedious process. Harry needed a spinning fullback, so he taught me this technique quickly. A few years later, when I was getting ready to coach, he taught me how to center. For many years I used those methods in teaching my own centers and fullbacks. Harry impressed on me that a coach must be able to teach the techniques used by any position player. Sure, you have good men as assistants, but sometimes they are not familiar with single wing techniques, so initially you may have to coach your coaches.

After I served in the Navy in the Pacific, I returned to Princeton in 1946 to play under Charlie Caldwell, the National Coach of the Year in 1950 and a Hall of Fame Coach. Charlie was excellent at planning a varied offense as he used all sorts of flankers and men-in-motion to dress up his basic unbalanced line single wing offense. As a quarterback in 1946, I sat in on strategy sessions with Charlie, and I will never forget how he illustrated varying his formation by moving checkers around on a table. In my later career as a coach, I always wanted to vary my basic formation in ways that would make for a more effective offense, and I'm sure those early sessions with Charlie's checkers helped me immeasurably.

Charlie always emphasized the ground game. His buck-lateral series running attack was exceptional. But when he had a Heisman Trophy winner at tailback, he knew how to take to the air successfully too. No single wing coach has ever been more successful with the running pass thrown to three different receivers. In the 1951 season Dick Kazmaier, his triple-threat tailback, threw this pass to three receivers a total of 67 times and completed 47 of them for 639 yards and 14 touchdowns.

After Princeton I entered graduate school at the University of Pennsylvania, studying for my Ph.D. in English. I had hopes of playing football with the Philadelphia Eagles to pay for my expenses while going to graduate school. (In those days pro players usually had only one practice a day.) After some five weeks of preseason, I was cut and then began teaching English part-time at Penn while doing my graduate work. At that time the idea of coaching football seemed a remote possibility, as I aspired to be a university English professor.

But somehow the game of football has a way of catching up with you. I became an English tutor for some of the Penn football players and eventually helped out coaching kickers for the Penn varsity. Before the 1952 season, George Munger, the legendary head coach at Penn, asked me to be head freshman football coach. (At that time, freshmen were not eligible to play varsity football.)

I had an awful lot to learn in a short time to get ready for that season. In addition to coaching the freshmen, during varsity games I often sat on the bench with headphones to pass on information from the coaches spotting upstairs. At this time Penn was playing big-time football before crowds up to 78,000 spectators. In 1952 and 1953 Penn was second in the nation in home attendance. Only Ohio State drew more spectators. In 1953 Penn played Vanderbilt, Penn State, California, Ohio State, Navy, Michigan, Notre Dame, Army, and Cornell. Hardly a soft schedule.

George Munger was an outstanding single wing football coach who was later inducted into the College Hall of Fame. His players loved him and played hard for him. He was excellent at making decisions during a game. His overall record of 82 wins, 42 losses, and 10 ties speaks for itself.

In those two years at Penn under George, I learned a lot of football, but I learned more about handling people. He was adept at getting everybody to contribute to the total effort while seeming to stay behind the scenes. A

quotation attributed to an ancient Chinese philosopher best sums up George's capacity to organize and lead his staff and players:

A leader is best
when people barely know he exists.
Not so good
when people obey and acclaim him.
Worse when they despise him.
But of a good leader
who talks little
when this work is done
his aim fulfilled
they will say:
We did it ourselves.
—Lao-tse (c.565B.C.)

For two summers I worked in a boys' camp in New Hampshire where George was the camp director. During this time we had many discussions about football as well as life. Many of the things I learned have stayed with me throughout my coaching career. Technically, among many other things, George left me with an appreciation for using seam bucks and a career-long aversion to throwing flat passes from dropback to the wide side of the field.

My coaching of the Penn freshmen during the 1952 and 1953 seasons, I'm sure, left much to be desired, but fortunately I had two excellent assistants who had been outstanding football players at Penn. Looking back, I had a lot of enthusiasm but many deficiencies. For one thing, I had not yet learned to organize a practice efficiently, a skill I worked hard to develop later on. We ran a watered-down replica of the Penn varsity's single wing offense, which was a sound one. The thing I remember most about our freshman offense was the success we had with the reverse pass, scoring long touchdowns with that play against the Army and Navy plebes and the Penn State freshmen. I used reverse passes throughout my career. (See Chapter 6.)

The 1953 season was George Munger's last as he retired from coaching after 16 years as head coach at Penn. Since the course work for my doctorate was completed and I had only my dissertation to finish, it seemed like a good time for me to move on. I was happy to go to the Lawrenceville School as an English teacher and football coach. For two years I was an assistant to long-time Lawrenceville coach, Larry Tiihonen, with the understanding I would take over from him in the 1956 season.

In 1956 I became head coach at Lawrenceville, introducing the single wing and using the wide tackle 6 defense. We used the quick kick extensively, a practice I was to follow throughout my coaching career. I was greatly influenced in this regard by Bowden Wyatt, the head coach of Tennessee. I went to three clinics at which he spoke, and corresponded with a Tennessee assistant coach about things like the quick kick, the fullback wedge, and their running pass. I also met Coach Wyatt and talked with him personally at a number of clinics. In 1956, using a balanced line single wing offense, Bowden Wyatt was the National Coach of the Year.

The first five seasons at Lawrenceville were to me a golden era. We had a wonderful group of kids to work with, and it was a time when young people were not cynical or jaded. They would willingly respond to the ideas of unity, hard work, and self-sacrifice. By 1958 we were running a good full spin series, and we ran well outside on end runs with excellent blocking. We were also able to vary our basic formation successfully with fullback flankers and especially with end over. We had great student leadership, which is the prerequisite of any success in football, a fact I have never forgotten. In 1958, 1959, and 1960 we went

undefeated, and when I was asked to come to Wabash College as head coach, I accepted, not knowing anything about the Wabash players or their opponents.

It is interesting to read the account of the Wabash College president, Byron Trippet, and the athletic director, Pete Vaughan, about their search for a new football coach. Years later in his memoirs, *Wabash On My Mind*, President Trippet wrote the following account:

Pete talked with all candidates we seriously considered. I investigated Ken Keuffel, head football coach at the Lawrenceville School. I immediately liked Ken. The idea of appointing a Ph.D. in English as football coach appealed to me and so did the notion of seeing the single wing style of football instituted at Wabash. After Ken's visit to Crawfordsville I asked Pete what he thought. He chuckled. "Well, he's sure different," he said. "But he is a very smart student of the game, and brother, does he have enthusiasm! The kids would like him. I think he would be pretty good." We appointed Ken Keuffel football coach.

Looking back, I am amazed at my confidence going into that job. Wabash had not had a winning season for four years. Furthermore, I had to assemble a staff and pull everything together in a short time. I guess I was too ignorant to be frightened. In any event, our single wing did well at Wabash. We had a wonderful group of spirited, courageous players, and many of our opponents were not familiar with the basic single wing offense, let alone maneuvers like the off-tackle jump pass or reverse passes. Early on, when we had undermanned squads, we were especially dependent upon the quick kick to make our opponents come a long way to score.

In my time at Wabash I met two other men who should be mentioned here: Clarence Stasavich, a highly successful single wing coach at Lenoir-Rhyne and East Carolina, and Keith Piper, the legendary single wing coach from

Denison. Both men were helpful to me, and they also assisted countless high school coaches.

In the summer of 1965, I spoke at a single wing clinic at East Carolina directed by Clarence Stasavich. Stas and I had exchanged films since his days at Lenoir-Rhyne, and I was honored to speak at his clinic and eager to learn from other coaches in attendance. Having just completed an 8-1 regular season capped by a 14-13 victory over the University of Massachusetts in the Tangerine Bowl, Stas had a loyal following of single wing coaches.

I am indebted to him for his advice on the passing game. Stas also taught me a good bit about the way to study films. He was a staunch believer in the unbalanced line single wing offense.

When I first met Keith Piper about 1963, he was using the balanced line single wing, but he had his greatest success at Denison later on with the unbalanced line attack. No one ever gave opposing defensive coaches more problems. His single wing offense featured a bewildering mixture of flankers and men-in-motion. Keith had many innovative ideas. I've always enjoyed watching his game films.

Wabash is a wonderful small college with high academic standards and great tradition. Even though I worked hard on football and recruiting, I was also able to teach a seminar in English one day a week in the off-season. The people at Wabash made a big thing about having a Ph.D. in English as head football coach, but I was well aware that to keep alumni and the community happy we had to win games. Fortunately we had no losing seasons, and my six years in Crawfordsville, Indiana, were among the happiest of my life. If it were not for the fact that recruiting is so important in college coaching, I might have stayed at Wabash. But I did not want to spend the rest of my life for half of each year on the road. It would have been the same situation at other colleges.

In 1967 I returned to Lawrenceville School as head coach and teacher of English. Lawrenceville was still a great school, but the climate in the country was changing to an unfortunate period of unrest and rebellion. This is no news to any teacher or coach who lived through the era of the Vietnam War and its aftermath. For a time it felt much harder to connect with the kids on important things when their interest often seemed to focus on styles of clothing, the length of one's hair, and overall recalcitrance. We had some outstanding football teams in the late sixties and seventies, but it was difficult to be consistent year after year.

I continued to work hard at the game, attending clinics and studying films. I can't remember a family vacation in which I didn't have my projector with me. There was always time for a couple of hours of film analysis. Coaches who teach academic subjects during the school year have to make time for football during vacations.

At this time I was influenced by the fullback in motion to the weakside attack, first developed by John Stiegman at Rutgers and later refined by Dick Colman at Princeton. I also toyed briefly with Dick's I-formation look, in which the tailback would line up directly in front of the fullback within the standard single wing formation.

Dick Colman was an excellent single wing football coach. I had played under him when he was an assistant to Charlie Caldwell, and we were good friends. We talked a lot of football, and I studied many of his game films. Succeeding Coach Caldwell, Dick was never given the credit he deserved. Over a 12-year span his teams won 75 games and lost only 33 for an outstanding winning percentage of .694, exactly the same as his predecessor. Both men were top coaches.

Through this period the greatest advance technically in my football was placing the tailback and fullback in three different horizontal positions so I could incorporate a more versatile offense. I discuss these features in later chapters of this book.

During these years we tended to use fewer basic plays and more variations, such as flankers and end over. We also designed plays with fewer pulling linemen. When we had tailbacks and wingbacks with good passing ability, we threw the ball more than we had in Wabash years. Thinking back on my time at Wabash, we could have used more passing.

Throughout my time at Wabash and later, I visited or corresponded with some outstanding single wing coaches, most of whom had retired from active coaching when I met up with them. I corresponded with Carl Snavely, a Hall of Fame coach who had great success at Cornell and North Carolina. We had several sessions of film analysis together. I'm sure some of his ideas stayed with me. I also spent many hours looking at single wing films, of other teams and my own teams, with John Stiegman, the former coach at Rutgers and Penn.

During this period I talked with, or corresponded with, some of the great single wing names of the past: Lou Little (Columbia), Tuss McLaughry (Dartmouth), Fritz Crisler (Michigan), Bernie Bierman (Minnesota), and Matty Bell (SMU). I'm sure I was a real pest to some of these people, but I valued what they could tell me about the single wing.

In 1982 I retired from coaching although I continued to teach English. I was about to turn 60 years old and figured it was time to do other things. During this period I continued to direct the Hall of Fame Clinic at Lawrenceville each year, so I was not divorced from football. Among the speakers I was fortunate to have eight coaches of college teams who went to bowls, including Joe Paterno and Frank

Beamer. Among top professional coaches were Dick Vermeil and Bill Belichick.

I continued to attend football clinics and visit college spring practice sessions. But what did the most to keep me involved with the game was looking at football films, especially old single wing films. Over time I had collected a sizable number of films from colleges that had given up the single wing and from other sources. More importantly, my good friend Ed Racely kept me supplied with many more. Ed probably has the largest collection of single wing films in the country. (We have since transferred most of our films to tape.)

You can learn a lot from looking at films of your own games and those of other single wing coaches. But of all the ideas I've picked up from film analysis, the one that sticks in my memory most vividly was a pass pattern taken from the Winged-T offense of Coach Frank Broyles of Arkansas about 1965. This eventually was transformed into our Option Trans, a play that has won many games for us. (See Chapter 8.)

Of the many films of single wing teams I have viewed, the following stand out: Carl Snavely's 1939 Cornell team that upset Ohio State 23-14; Charlie Caldwell's 1950 and 1951 Princeton teams with Dick Kazmaier; George Munger's 1952 and 1953 Penn teams; John Stiegman's 1958 Rutgers team with Bill Austin; Dick Colman's 1964 Princeton team with Cosmo Iacavazzi; Fritz Crisler's 1939 Michigan team with Tom Harmon and his last Michigan team that finished undefeated with a 49-0 Rose Bowl victory on January 1, 1948.

In 1990 I became head coach at Lawrenceville for the third time. The next 10 seasons were fun. A special treat was having the sons of a number of former players on my teams. I hadn't realized how much I missed coaching.

What I especially appreciated about the players on these teams was their positive attitude. Regardless of their ability, these boys bought into the ideas of hard work and team play in a way that was highly gratifying. I was older than some of their grandfathers, but there was no generation gap. Football players today will respond to the same things they did 50 years ago: motivation, encouragement, organization, and discipline. These are things they often don't get elsewhere.

During this period, when we had players with ability, we had some excellent football teams. Homer Smith, the captain of Charlie Caldwell's 1953 Princeton team and later head coach at Army and offensive coordinator at UCLA and Alabama, viewed a tape of one of our better teams. Of this Lawrenceville team, he wrote: *Your offense looked as good as Princeton's ever looked. The power off-tackle, the half spin, the smooth reverses, the Statue of Liberty (even off the quick kick), the running pass, the cross action pass, the throwback—it was beautiful.* I am grateful to Homer for writing this letter, which was dated August 7, 2000.

After the 1999 season I retired from coaching football at the age of 76. I've had a deeply satisfying career that has brought me a great deal of pleasure. If given the opportunity, I would do it all over again.

Over the years I have worked with many fine men who served as assistant coaches and many wonderful boys who played on my teams. Because it would not be possible to name them all, I have not named any of them in this book. I treasure their memories, all of them.

Chapter 2

SETTING UP an OFFENSE

Football is not a simple game. But if a coach can set up a clear and well-organized system of offense, he's made a start at gaining coaching success. Every player must be able to understand what play it is, his assignment on the play, and how that play dovetails with any related plays. For many years the overall organization of our offense has worked very well. I hope other single wing coaches can get some ideas here that will help them in organizing their offensive systems.

In this chapter there are sections on the placement of players in proper positions, designing a clear and concise system, devising an efficient method of numbering plays, recognizing the important role of the center in our offensive plan, designating variations of the basic formation, and huddle procedure and the signal system in actual use. These matters are of great importance in setting up an efficient single wing offensive system.

Placement and Numbering of Players

We line up our basic single wing offense in the manner diagramed in Figures 1 and 2. In one diagram we are set up in right formation; in the other, in left formation. Each lineman is given a number. These numbers identify each position and usually signify where a running

RIGHT FORMATION
(With Numbered Linemen)

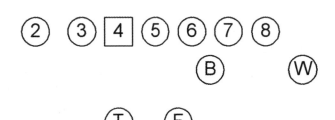

Figure 1

LEFT FORMATION
(With Numbered Linemen)

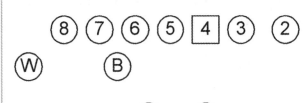

Figure 2

13

play will end up. The center is No. 4. The other interior linemen are referred to as No. 3, No. 5, No. 6, and No. 7. We do not have guards or tackles. The No. 8 end is also referred to as the strongside end; the No. 2 end, as the weakside end.

Our five interior linemen, from the No. 3 to the No. 7, have only minimum splits of a few inches between them. We say they split "for comfort." The No. 8 end is normally split 1 foot from the No. 7, and the No. 2 end is usually split 2 or 3 feet from the No. 3, though obviously in sure passing situations or in other special circumstances they may want to be out a bit wider.

The tailback and fullback line up at a depth of 4 to 5 yards about a yard apart. The tailback will line up in one of three positions: Far, behind the No. 3 lineman; Near, behind the center; Close, left foot on the ball in right formation (right foot on the ball in left formation). This seems complicated, but it is really simple in operation: The tailback knows he always lines up in the same place on a given play (e.g., Far position on Play No. 48, Near position on Play No. 49). Throughout this book I give a Far or Near or Close position for each play discussed. These positions are helpful in running our offense.

The wingback usually lines up about 2 feet outside the strongside end and about 2 feet behind him. The blocking back usually lines up behind the seam between the No. 6 lineman and No. 7 lineman at about 1-yard depth.

In both right and left formations each player takes the same position relative to his teammates. In both formations he has the same assignment on any given play.

Player Selection for Different Positions

As in the case of all offensive systems, we must select players for the different positions

who are best fitted to do the jobs we will ask of them. We attempt to place a boy in his proper position just as soon as possible. But sometimes we guess wrong as to his capabilities or we are forced to move him to another position because of personnel shortages elsewhere. Ideally a boy will be placed in a suitable position from the first day of practice so he can learn just as much as possible about playing that position. A brief description of the requirements for each position follows:

The Center

The first position you must provide for in a single wing offense is the Center (No. 4). He should be a good-sized boy who can be taught to center accurately and block at least adequately. He need not be fast and actually in many respects he can be only an average athlete. But he must be a steady, persevering type of player who will work hard to perfect the skills required of him.

Most years our center has been a one-way player who does not play on defense. Unlike some other single wing teams, we do not ask him to do much more than center the football accurately on various types of passes and carry out limited blocking assignments.

By using the simple drills discussed in Chapter 3, we have had little trouble developing competent centers in a short time—both in high school and college coaching. Any boy who can already throw some sort of a spiral pass for a short distance will generally have the manual dexterity to become a center. He must practice his snapping a great deal in individual drills to gain confidence before having to snap when the team runs actual plays. He should have plenty of practice in the off-season.

Other Linemen

Over the years in coaching schoolboys, we have developed a way to take advantage of the different physical abilities of our interior linemen. Some players are asked to do more difficult tasks than others, depending on their position.

The No. 6 should be a good straight-ahead blocker with considerable speed. He pulls to block outside to the strongside on Play No. 49 (our end run) and on Play No. 79 (our basic running pass), in addition to other plays. He also pulls to the weakside on some plays.

No. 7 must be a big boy who is a good shoulder-blocker with enough speed to pull through the hole and block a backer on our 3-hole plays (inside reverses).

In the present system, our No. 5 can be a heavy boy with little speed who can block well on seam bucks and wedge plays. We no longer ask him to pull and trap.

Our No. 3 must have quickness because he pulls on certain plays, but we no longer ask him to do much trapping. He can be a smaller boy than the other interior linemen.

Ends (No. 8 and No. 2). In selecting our ends we are governed pretty much by the same criteria as those coaches using other offensive systems. We like our ends to be good pass receivers and blockers. Usually they are fairly tall. We ask our ends to execute the various post-and-power blocks, common to any lineman in our offense. We also involve them in a good bit of open-field blocking on linebackers and secondary defensive men.

In theory, our No. 8 or strongside end should be the better close-up shoulder-blocker, and the No. 2 or weakside end the better open-field blocker and pass receiver. Therefore, if we have a bigger and more powerful end, he will usually be placed on the strongside, while a faster but smaller boy who is a good pass receiver will probably be on the weakside. However, anytime we can find two big ends who are both excellent blockers and pass receivers, we will place them at different end spots and play them both at the same time.

Backfield Positions

Wingback

In choosing our wingbacks we look first for a boy with speed and ball-carrying ability. Usually he will be one of our fastest backs because without speed at wingback we cannot operate our reverses successfully. Because we look for speed first at this position, we often have to be satisfied with smaller boys.

The wingback should also be a good blocker and, if possible, an excellent pass receiver. In addition, it is most helpful if he is a passer because we have several effective reverse passes in our attack. Whenever we can find a left-handed passer who can also do the other jobs we expect of our wingbacks, we know we will have an excellent threat with our reverse passes from right formation.

Blocking Back

When we are looking for a blocking back, we look first for an articulate boy who is a leader. He is our quarterback. And though we send in plays from the bench, we want him to be decisive in the huddle and forceful when barking out signals at the line of scrimmage. Next we look for blocking ability since this player is required to execute many of the key blocks in our offensive system. In addition, we hope to have boys at this position who are at least adequate pass receivers because we feel that the short optional running pass to the blocking back is one of the strongest plays in football.

Fullback

In selecting a fullback we look for a rugged boy who has quickness and speed, blocking ability in the open field, and some skill as a power runner. He obviously should have good size for a backfield man and above-average coordination and athletic ability.

Tailback

We expect a tailback to be either a good runner and an adequate passer, or at least an average runner and a first-rate passer. We do not demand that he perform both skills in extraordinary fashion. In addition, it is helpful though not essential that the tailback also quick-kick reasonably well, a skill most boys of this type can develop. Clearly our tailbacks will be among our better athletes.

Method of Numbering Running Plays

We number our offensive linemen so we can direct where a play will go. The last digit of any running play designates the offensive man over whose general area the play will be run. Thus any play ending with 8 will be run somewhere in the area of the No. 8, the strongside end. For wide plays we use 9 on the strongside and 1 on the weakside.

The first digit of any play describes exactly the type of center that will be made. A 4 center, for example, is a lead center to a spot about 2 feet to the side of the tailback and at a height slightly above the knees.

OFF-TACKLE (PLAY NO. 48)

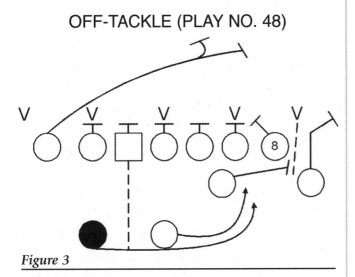

Figure 3

The numbering of Play No. 48 tells our players, then, that this play will start out with a certain type of lead center to the tailback and end up over the general area of No. 8, the strongside end. Figure 3 illustrates this play, which is easily recognizable as our off-tackle play. The assignments for all players are given in detail in Chapter 4.

INSIDE REVERSE (PLAY NO. 43)

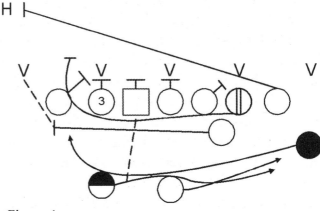

Figure 4

Play No. 43 indicates that again there is a 4 center, but this time the play ends up over the general area of No. 3 on an inside reverse to the wingback. (See Figure 4.)

FULLBACK SEAM BUCK (PLAY NO. 16)

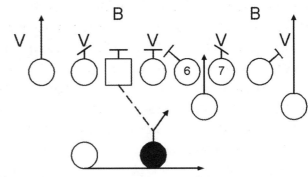

Figure 5

A 1 center is a soft lob pass to the fullback. Thus Play No. 16 indicates the fullback will run a seam buck in the general area of No. 6. (See Figure 5.)

TAILBACK SEAM BUCK (PLAY NO. 56)

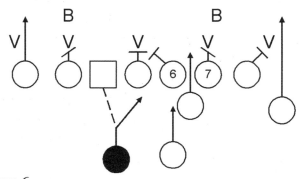

Figure 6

When we want our tailback to run a seam buck (behind the fullback) we give the tail a 1 center but designate the first digit as 5. Thus Play No. 56 indicates the tailback runs a buck in the general area of No. 6. (See Figure 6.)

The Center and Different Offensive Cycles

We are always careful to make things as clear as possible to the center. That is why we number the types of center passes we use. It is a great help to our centers to be able to pair up and practice their exact types of passes in a specialty period before practice or at other times.

We have already seen that a 4 center describes a lead center to the tailback and a 1 center is a soft lob center hung out in front of the fullback. Now I will describe other kinds of centers.

A 2 center indicates a pass to the outside knee of the fullback (i.e., to his right knee in right formation) so he can make a half spin to the wingback, while the tailback runs directly toward the weakside. He may give to the wingback, or fake to the wingback and carry the ball himself.

A 3 center signifies a pass to the inside knee of the fullback so he can spin toward the tailback. On a 30 series play the fullback may

either give to the tailback or he may fake to the tailback and give to the wingback, or he may fake to one or both backs and then carry the ball himself. The mechanics of the full spin are discussed in Chapter 3. We have seen that a 1 center can be given a 5 as the first digit on seam bucks when the tailback carries.

A 6 center is a direct pass to the tailback, who can either pass or fake a pass and run with the ball himself.

INSIDE REVERSE (PLAY NO. 43)

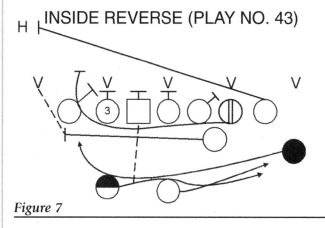

Figure 7

FULLBACK HALF SPIN (PLAY NO. 23)

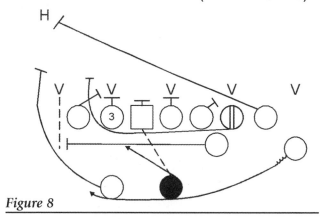

Figure 8

FULLBACK FULL SPIN (PLAY NO. 33)

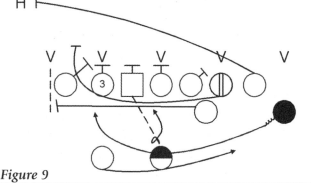

Figure 9

An 8 center is a pass to the outside knee of the tailback so he can half-spin to the fullback and either give him the ball or carry the ball himself.

Our 3 hole will demonstrate how the same basic blocking can be used on three different plays: 43, 23, and 33. (See Figures 7, 8, and 9.) For any 3-hole play, all linemen and the blocking back will have the same assignments although the backfield men will execute different maneuvers. Later in the book we'll see that 3-hole blocking is also used on Plays 63, 63 shovel, and 83. We never carried six 3-hole plays in our attack at any one time, but this system gives us the flexibility to add plays quickly as needed.

Method of Designating Pass Plays

For dropback passes, we describe the pattern, and the center makes a straight-back pass to the tailback, who aligns in close position and drops back behind No. 5, the middle offensive lineman. Here is 2 end cross pass. (See Figure 10.)

2 END CROSS PASS

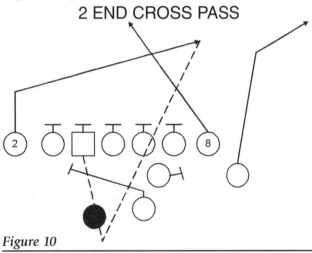

Figure 10

On dropback pass plays, we use only one protection and describe the pattern. Also we usually name the preferred receiver: e.g., 2 end cross, Quick 8 hook. These plays and other patterns are covered in detail in Chapter 6.

We use a 4 center on 79, our basic running pass to the strongside and on all running pass

variations, which are designated by 99. Play No. 79 is diagramed in Figure 11. The final digit is 9, indicating the play, which can turn into a run, ends up in the wide area to the strongside. All these passes are discussed in Chapter 6.

RUNNING PASS (PLAY NO. 79)

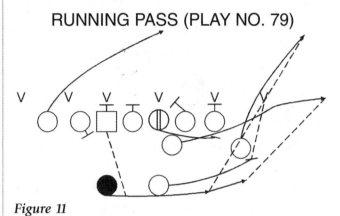

Figure 11

Using Variations of Formation

We are completely sold on the importance of occasionally varying our basic single wing formation. For this reason we use different kinds of flankers, men-in-motion, split ends, and ends over. In Chapter 8, I will explain in detail how such variations can be used effectively.

For any one game we may want to utilize only several of these variations, but the blocking back in the huddle must still be able to designate them just as clearly and concisely as he does his running plays and passes. If there is confusion in the minds of any team member as to just how the variations are to be set up and implemented, we will lose more than we gain by using them.

In designating variations of the formation, we refer to backs and ends either by name or number. The two numbers used are 3 for the fullback and 4 for the tailback. Flank indicates a flanker to the strongside, whether right or left formation; X designates a flanker to the weakside. Thus we called 3 flank and 3X for the fullback, and 4 flank and 4X for the tailback. For 3X see Figure 12. Variations 3 Move and 4 Move would indicate that either player went in motion to the weakside.

FULLBACK FLANKER TO WEAKSIDE (3X)

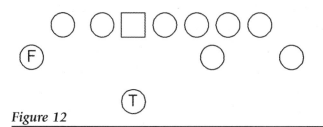

Figure 12

Zip indicates the tail and full change places when they line up, whether in right or left formation. (See Figure 13.) The Zip suggests with this variation we can get more quickly to the weakside on certain plays.

TAIL AND FULL CHANGE PLACES (ZIP)

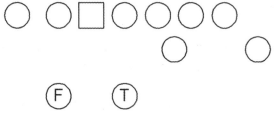

Figure 13

Variation A means the wingback is set wide to the strongside. Variation B indicates the wingback is set wide or close to the weakside. Over the years we have used both A and B extensively to spread opposing defenses.

With end variations we use expressive terminology rather than numbers. Again, it is understood that all variations are with reference to the strongside or weakside, regardless of whether we are in right or left formation.

Split means the weakside end is split out wide. This is by design of the play. At other times, on certain plays, the end has leeway to flex or split out on his own. Slot means the strongside end is aligned wide outside the wingback like Army's old "lonesome end."

END OVER ALIGNMENT

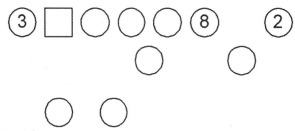

Figure 14

End Over means the weakside end is aligned close outside the wingback. (See Figure 14.) End Over Wide indicates the weakside end is set up wide outside the wingback. Swap is a variation of End Over with the No. 2 end still on the weakside as the eligible receiver. (See Figure 15.)

SWAP ALIGNMENT

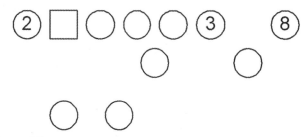

Figure 15

I want to emphasize again that for any one game we will use only a few variations, which we have been practicing all week. And these variations don't change the assignments of most players on basic plays. So using variations intelligently can pose difficult problems for the opposing team without requiring much preparation time.

Following is a summary of the designations for the variations we have most often used:

For Backfield Men

Zip: tailback and fullback change places

Flank: flanker to strongside

X: flanker to weakside

Move: motion to weakside

Q: blocking back set behind No. 3 lineman

A: wingback set wide to strongside

B: wingback set wide or close to weakside

For Ends

Slot: strongside end aligned wide outside wingback

Split: weakside end split wide

End Over: weakside end aligned close out-side wingback

Swap: a variation of End Over with the No. 2 end still on the weakside

End Over Wide: weakside end aligned wide out-side wingback

These variations are not used in haphazard fashion. Each one has a purpose. It is difficult for most opponents to defense the basic single wing formation. The use of variations exacerbates their problems.

Huddle Procedure and the Signal System in Use

In actual use the various parts of the signal system can be fitted together easily. In the huddle the blocking back, our quarterback, calls the formation (right or left), the play number, and the starting count. Typical examples would be Right 48, on 1 and Left 21 pass, on 2. (48 is shorthand for Play No. 48; 21 Pass, for Play No. 21 Pass.)

If any variation of the formation is desired, this information comes immediately after the Right or Left call. Typical examples would be Right 3X, 43, on 1 and Left A, 16, on 1.

We use a rhythmic cadence as an aid to our center. It would be difficult for a single wing center to make his various types of center passes with a nonrhythmic starting cadence.

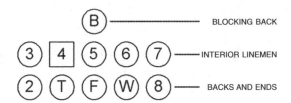

Figure 16

We have an open huddle with the interior linemen in the front row and the backs and ends in the back row. (See Figure 16.) The linemen assume a comfortable position with their hands on their knees. The backs and ends in the rear row stand in a comfortable position behind the linemen. The center sets the position for the huddle by lining up 6 or 7 yards from the football. This arrangement discourages unnecessary talking in the huddle.

We usually send in plays by players as messengers or by signaling. In addition, if the blocking back is close to the bench, I'll often yell in a play. The blocking back, standing in front of the huddle, has his back to the line of scrimmage during the brief time he does any talking. The other players face the opponent's goal line.

In the huddle, the blocking back calls the formation (right or left), the play, and the starting count. Then the center will leave the huddle. While the center is running up and adjusting the ball, the blocking back repeats the complete information he gave before. Then he barks out "Ready, Break," and the entire team will give a clap of their hands and run up to their positions on the line of scrimmage.

So he does not get run over, the blocking back steps into the center's vacated area as he yells "Ready, Break." (This command is for right formation plays.)

If it is a right formation play, which it is about two thirds of the time, all players only have to move forward to take their numbered positions. If it is a left formation play, the blocking back will bark rhythmically "Ends, Ready, Break." On hearing "Ends," the ends start crossing behind the huddle. On "Break" all players clap their hands and the No. 7 leads the other linemen diagonally across and up to align themselves on the center, while the backs delay for a second before setting up behind them in left formation.

Using this serpentine method of leaving the huddle in left formation allows us to see at a glance whether or not the defensive players are using the flop-over plan. That is, whether they line up in the same position relative to the strength of the offense versus formation left or right. In the chapter on offensive strategy, I will discuss the advantages and disadvantages of this defensive plan and how we can exploit it.

When the players get to the line of scrimmage in right or left formation, they assume a comfortable stationary position with their hands on their knees. The blocking back then barks the command "Team Get Down!" and each player takes his normal stance. It is important that all players remain stationary for at least one second before this command because we will sometimes run a play from an up position on "Down." This can be highly effective because the defense may not be set on an early count.

After all players have gotten down, the No. 8 end will call "Even" if there is a man head-on him, or "Odd" if there is no man head-on him. He makes these calls on every play. They help the players on the strongside of our formation get oriented.

The blocking back will pause for a few seconds before beginning the following rhythmic cadence: "Red, Set, Hut, Hut, Hut." (We start with Red because our nickname is "Big Red.") The ball may occasionally be snapped on "Set," but it is usually snapped on one of the first three "Huts."

In the interest of simplicity, a 20 number play will be snapped on "two," the second "Hut"; a 30 number play on "Three," the third "Hut"; and other plays on "one," the first "Hut." All quick kicks and fake quick kicks will go on "Three."

It is important to have efficient huddle procedure. All members of a team must break from the huddle and line up with precision and enthusiasm or it will not be possible to achieve the kind of team take-off that is necessary for a successful offense. Teams that are sloppy or lethargic at these times are apt to play that way after the ball is snapped.

Conclusion

The basic organization of any offense must be well planned in every detail. This organization covers the placement and selection of personnel, a clear and comprehensive signal system, blocking adjustments to cope with different defenses, and orderly and efficient huddle procedure. These elements are vital to the success of any offense.

Chapter 3

Teaching Individual POSITION PLAY

In our unbalanced line single wing, as in other offensive systems, there are certain basic techniques that must be mastered by individual players if our team maneuvers are to be successful. In this chapter I will discuss the most important of these fundamentals, outlining the drills used to teach them. I will place particular emphasis on characteristic single wing techniques, such as those of the center and the tailback, which are not used in other offensive systems. This discussion should be especially helpful to high school coaches.

Techniques of Center Play

A dependable center is the key to any single wing offense. You will not have an effective attack if this boy cannot learn to pass the ball accurately. But centering the football, as important as that is, is not his only job. He also has blocking assignments to carry out. And because he must have his head down to pass the ball, our center will have certain problems that are not encountered in other offenses.

There are three aspects to be considered in the play of the center in our system. One has to do with his stance. Another is concerned

with the mechanics of centering the football. A third has to do with the center's techniques of blocking after the pass.

FRONT VIEW OF CENTER

Figure 17

23

SIDE VIEW OF CENTER

Figure 18

KNOCKING KNEES TO OUTSIDE

Figure 19

Stance

Figures 17 and 18 show front and side views of the center when he is about to pass the football. In taking his stance, the center should assume a comfortably wide base with feet parallel.

To insure a wide range of vision and freedom of arm movement while passing the ball, the knees should be as wide as comfort allows. When teaching this body position to an inexperienced center, a helpful practice is to have the boy bend over and knock his knees to the outside with his elbows several times before placing his hands on the football. (See Figure 19.)

Some coaches have advocated that one foot should be slightly in front of the other. Unless this seems natural to a boy, we prefer to have him take his stance with the feet about even.

Notice that in the photographs the center's head is over the football. This position will vary somewhat with an individual's length of arms and body build. The important point to emphasize with a beginner is that the head will not be behind the football as is the case with his teammates on either side, who naturally cannot encroach on the neutral zone when lining up.

Teaching the Beginning Center

The methods we use in teaching beginners to center a football have been successful in both high school and college coaching. I am sure some of the best teaching we do is in this phase of play.

We normally begin working with inexperienced centers by having them pair up and toss a football back and forth at a distance of no more than 10 yards. They throw the ball to each other easily in normal overhand passing fashion. This allows them to warm up and get the proper feel of throwing a spiral pass, with the ball going off the tips of the first two fingers in the same manner as regular passers throw the ball.

BEGINNING CENTER'S DRILL

Figure 20

Next we have each boy turn around and throw one-handed spiral passes to his partner from between his legs at a distance of about 5 yards. (See Figure 20.) Though this motion somewhat resembles a centering technique, the ball is not placed on the ground. As shown in the photograph, the boy bends over just far enough to see his target from between his legs.

The next step is to place the ball on the ground and throw a one-handed spiral pass between the legs. At this stage no effort is made to assume a proper stance, and the nonthrowing hand can hang down in a relaxed fashion.

Only after completing these progressive drills will we have a beginner take the wide stance described above and place both hands on the football. At this time we will show him the grip we want used, but he is still made to feel that centering will be a natural extension of the easy one-handed passing he has been doing. You can develop a competent center after surprisingly little practice time if he believes his job is not difficult.

Technique of Centering the Football

The center places the ball on the ground with the laces directly underneath the middle of the ball. Assuming a right-handed center, he grips the ball with his right hand exactly as he would on a regular pass. The wrist is slightly cocked as in the earlier drills. The left hand is placed lightly on the left-hand side of the ball.

The right hand applies the major impetus to the spiraling football while the left hand helps to control the flight of the ball as both hands follow through together on the pass with a smooth, flowing motion. He feels both hands are flowing to the target.

The center must make sure to bend over low, have his feet parallel, and knock his knees out. He can't do the job if he doesn't assume a proper stance. He must practice, practice, practice. For a while he should not worry about the different types of center passes mentioned in Chapter 2 but should concentrate on stance, manual control, and straight-back centering.

Blocking After the Pass

Compared to his T-formation counterpart, who can keep his head up while passing the ball, our single wing center will obviously be somewhat handicapped in his blocking. Therefore he must learn to snap his head up and get into position to block as quickly as possible. He should never delay to see whether his pass was accurate because he will not be able to recover a loose ball anyway.

Usually our center's blocking assignment calls for him to snap his head up and be in a position to shoulder-block a defensive lineman in his immediate area. On any blocking of this sort, except a simple check block to the offside, he will get help from a teammate.

Basic Techniques of Other Linemen

Though the techniques we teach our centers are not used in most other offensive systems, this is not the case with our other linemen. On many T-formation teams today the linemen are taught the same basic stance we use, plus many of the same fundamentals of shoulder-blocking, double teaming, pulling, and trapping.

Stance

The first prerequisite of good line play is a proper stance. Except for the center, all of our linemen are taught the same basic stance, which we consider to be a balanced one. This is necessary because all of our linemen have assignments that require them to move quickly in several different directions.

Figures 21 and 22 show the basic stance we teach our linemen. As can be seen, this is a staggered stance with the feet at about shoulder width, pointing straight ahead, and one foot slightly in front of the other. The distance one foot should be in front of the other cannot be rigidly fixed since it will vary considerably with the body build of individual players.

If the left foot is forward, the right hand will be down, touching the ground with either the knuckles or the fingers. There should be little, if any, weight on the extended hand to allow the lineman to move in different directions without offering tip-offs. The arm that is not extended should be placed across the thigh in a relaxed position.

The head should be up, with the eyes looking straight ahead. The back should be straight.

LINEMAN'S STANCE - FRONT VIEW

Figure 21

LINEMAN'S STANCE - SIDE VIEW

Figure 22

The hips should be slightly lower than the shoulders. The shoulders should be almost level, though the side of the extended arm will naturally be slightly lower.

Shoulder Block

The basic block our linemen use is the shoulder block. Starting from his three-point stance, the lineman executes the basic shoulder block by shooting his body forward and contacting his opponent with the flat surface of his shoulder and upper arm. Ordinarily he will step out with the right foot if he uses the right shoulder. However, the important element for the blocker is take-off speed, and his techniques cannot always be as planned because of the different defensive charges he will encounter.

At the moment of shoulder contact the head should be up and pinching against the defensive man's body. The neck should be bulled and the back straight. The blocker should feel he is exploding through his opponent as he takes short, choppy steps from a wide base.

In practicing the shoulder block we have the boys do a great deal of individual work against both blocking dummies and the blocking sled. When conducting these drills you must make sure the linemen practice blocking as much with the left shoulder as the right. If not instructed to do differently, our right-handed players invariably seem to hit with the right shoulder much more than with the left, and the left-handers just the opposite. Since they will probably have to block an equal number of times with both shoulders in actual games, they should certainly do the same in practice.

Many inexperienced players try to execute the shoulder block with their legs too close together. A drill we have found particularly helpful in developing the necessary wide base is what we call the board drill. For this drill we use a board about 8 to 10 feet long and 12 inches wide. One player holds the dummy upright at one end of the board and guides it while the blocker drives the dummy down to the other end. Because his feet straddle the board, the blocker is forced into using a wide stance. This drill takes little time, but I think it is extremely beneficial.

Along with these drills for form and technique, we have the linemen practice using the shoulder block under live conditions in the one-on-one drill. Two boys line up opposite each other with one on offense and one on defense. The coach stands behind the defensive man and signals which shoulder the offensive man will use on his block. You should instruct the defensive man to charge straight ahead into the other boy. This basic drill is one of our best.

Double Team Block

The basic double team block is a combination shoulder-blocking effort of two offensive men against one opposing lineman. This maneuver is often referred to as a post-and-power block.

On this block a lineman with a man opposite him (the post blocker) stops the charge of the opponent, and his adjacent teammate (the power blocker) drives the defensive man in a lateral direction down the line. At the instant the power blocker explodes into the defensive man from the side, the post swings his legs and hips in the direction of his teammate, sealing the seam between them. Then both men work together to drive their opponent in a lateral direction.

The techniques of the double team block can be practiced against a dummy held upright or in live contact. One of the best drills to teach this block is the two-on-one drill shown in Figure 23. The two offensive men can work together in either direction against the dummy or live defensive man opposite

TWO-ON-ONE DRILL

Figure 23

THREE-ON-ONE DRILL

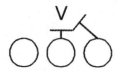

Figure 24

them. If the drill is run as live contact, the coach stands behind the defensive man to indicate to the two offensive men the direction in which the double team block should be applied.

The three-on-one drill shown in Figure 24 is best used under live conditions. Again the coach stands behind the defensive man to indicate the type and direction of block to be made. He may indicate a double team block to the right or to the left or a wedge (triple team). Naturally on a double team the middle man will be the post and an outside man the power blocker. On a wedge, all three men will shoot out together.

Though we are here discussing the last two drills from the offensive standpoint, it goes without saying they can be used for teaching defensive play too. This is also true of the other live contact drills mentioned in this section.

Dropback Pass Protection

Many of our best passes are either running passes or reverse passes, which are based on the fakes of running plays. But we also throw many passes from dropback action, and the linemen must be drilled on this protection, both individually and as a unit. We use the same techniques that are used in other styles of offense. The protector jolts the defensive man with his arms, then stays on balance for repeated blows. This basic technique is also used on protection for quick kicks.

Pulling

All of our linemen are taught to pull because this maneuver leads to so many of the blocking assignments in our offense. A man may pull to trap an opposing lineman. He may pull through a hole to block an opposing backer. He may pull wide to lead a sweep. He may pull to protect behind the line on passes. He may pull to influence a defensive man playing opposite him, that is, make that man think it will be an outside play and thus set him up for a trap from the inside.

Learning to pull correctly demands a good bit of attention to detail. However, I can hardly think of a player we have coached in high school or college who could not learn this skill reasonably well after some practice time.

Starting from the stance I discussed, the lineman will begin by taking a short lateral lead step in the direction he is pulling. Assuming he is pulling to the right, he will pivot on the ball of the left foot while swinging his body around about 90 degrees to plant the right foot. Pumping his right arm backward will help him pivot quickly.

After he plants his right foot, the pulling lineman will commence taking short steps, pumping his arms vigorously like a sprinter starting a race. He must be drilled to stay low throughout his pull, which with practice will become one smoothly flowing operation.

Obviously a lineman must not tip off when he is going to pull by altering his stance. A natural tendency of inexperienced players is to lean noticeably in the direction they will be pulling.

Trapping

In our system a trap block is designed to be closely coordinated with a double team block. If a lineman does the trapping, he will make a shallow pull and shoulder-block the first defensive man who appears past the double team.

During the first few steps of his pull, the trapper must head up into the line toward a point where he can block his man no matter how little he penetrates. Then even if the defensive man shows good trap reaction and does not come past the line of scrimmage, the trapper can still scoop him out. If the defensive man penetrates some distance, it is relatively easy for the trapper to adjust to block him.

TRAPPING DRILL

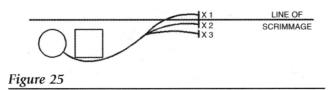

Figure 25

Figure 25 shows a drill we use to teach proper trapping techniques. The trapper pulls around another man (or a blocking dummy), runs up into the line, and adjusts to block a dummy held at positions 1, 2, or 3. If the dummy holder uses a light dummy, he can easily move to the position designated by the coach. This gives the trapper practice in adjusting to different defensive charges.

The trapper must always have his head to the inside so the defensive man cannot slide off his block in the direction of the ball carrier. In this case the trapper would always block with his right shoulder.

Pulling Through a Hole

Pulling through a hole is a maneuver that is often coordinated with double team and trap blocking. The lineman will precede the ball carrier through a hole to provide interference.

On this maneuver, the lineman pulls from the line as usual but makes sure to gain a bit of depth so as to be in position to turn through the hole. He must again stay low while running. As he turns through the hole, he should drop his inside shoulder and reach for the grass with that hand just in front of his inside foot. Once he reaches the hole, the pulling lineman will normally think first of turning to the inside to make his block though obviously he must take the first man he sees. We want him to use a running shoulder block.

Wingback Techniques

When we are dealing with offensive backfield play, there is a change in our teaching approach. Unlike the basic drills for linemen described above, we tend to use only a few drills for the backs in common. Instead we concentrate mainly on the techniques used by individual backs in the various plays and series of our offense. The play of the wingback offers a good example of this teaching approach. Again, I will mention here only those points that will not be covered in detailed explanations of the different plays in our offense.

Stance

Our wingback uses basically the same balanced stance as our offensive linemen. From this stance he must be able to pull deep into the backfield on reverses, release as a pass receiver, and block opposing linemen and linebackers. Sometimes his blocking assignment will require him to work with the strongside end as part of a double team on the defensive tackle, and sometimes it will mean a single block on a defensive end or linebacker.

Shoulder Block

All of our wingbacks must perfect the techniques of shoulder-blocking, described above for linemen. In addition to the board drill and to individual work on the dummies and the blocking sled, our wingbacks pair up with our strongside offensive ends to do a certain amount of live two-on-one practice against a defensive lineman. This is necessary or we will be in trouble when we encounter a defense in which the tackle plays head-on our strongside end. If our wingback cannot power-block a tackle in this position, we will not be able to run our off-tackle plays, which are so vital to our offense.

Blocking an Individual Man

When blocking a man head-on him or to his inside, the wingback attacks with a shoulder block, making sure not to leave his feet before contact. He must have his head on the outside. Under the present high school rules, he cannot block below the waist. If the wingback will make contact and keep battling, that is enough. He does not have to move the defensive man.

Pulling on Reverses

When the wingback runs a course into the backfield to accept the ball from the tailback or fullback on a reverse, he uses much the same technique as a lineman pulling out of the line.

The only difference is that the wingback's course will be deeper than the lineman's pull.

The wingback must gain a great deal of depth on his first two steps and then level off so he can accept the ball while running parallel to the line. Then he can turn downfield to hit the desired hole at a 90-degree angle. This can be practiced easily in skeleton backfield drills.

To teach the correct courses to our backs and to perfect the timing of our running plays, we frequently run skeleton backfield drills, utilizing the canvas strip shown in Figure 26. As can be seen in the photograph, numbers are painted on this strip to correspond to the positions of our numbered offensive linemen. In this way we can drill the backs and a center on the ball handling and timing of a play without involving the linemen, who can be working separately. Often we have two strips in use.

SKELETON BACKFIELD - USING STRIP

Figure 26

Blocking Back Techniques

The blocking back or quarterback in our system has two types of blocks to learn: the shoulder block and the pass protection block. He must have plenty of work on the board drill, the dummies, and the blocking sled. In addition, he must have practice in catching the running pass. Finally, he must have a good bit of drill in huddle procedure and calling cadence, subjects that are discussed in Chapter 2.

Stance

The blocking back uses a high two-point stance. (See photo of backfield stance, Figure 27.) The legs are spread with feet pointing forward and hands resting on the knees. This stance allows him to look over the defensive alignment before the play starts and to start quickly in a lateral direction on the snap.

In our system, it is not necessary for the blocking back to be able to start quickly going forward. When he does, he takes a quick backward false step and then runs forward as the fullback does on seam bucks. If a back does not use a false step, he will be leaning forward and pick up motion penalties.

Shoulder Block

For the various traps he must make on defensive ends and interior linemen, the blocking back uses the same shoulder-blocking techniques described above for linemen. Like any trapping lineman, he must first head up into the line so he can make an inside-out scoop on a defensive man who does not penetrate. Again he must have his head to the inside so the defensive man cannot easily slide off his block in the direction of the ball carrier.

When the fullback is to block the end from the outside on the running pass, the blocking back should run right up to the end before sliding out into the flat as a pass receiver. This technique of the blocking back helps set up the fullback's block on the end.

BACKFIELD STANCE

Figure 27

Fullback Techniques

In addition to his ball-carrying and blocking assignments, the fullback must learn certain other specialized offensive techniques that are not emphasized in other systems. These include diving over the top and either the half-spin or the full-spin maneuver. But above all, he must be a tough blocker and a strong straight-ahead runner.

Stance

The fullback and the tailback use a two-point stance similar to that of the blocking back. Figure 27 shows a good stance for the fullback or tailback. Both backs must have their eyes focused intently on the football. In our system the tailback and the fullback are the only backs in a position to take a direct pass from center. They both look at the ball before all plays so there will never be a tip-off as to which one will catch the ball.

Blocking Assignments

Like the blocking back, the fullback is a key blocker for us. Because of the high school rules that prohibit blocking below the waist on the outside, the fullback can no longer use the long body block. However, he can still block a defensive end effectively on outside plays if he uses proper techniques.

He should approach the defensive man under control, using short steps, and make a tackle on that man without using his arms. Actually he uses a running shoulder block, and the tailback cuts off his block.

The fullback must also be a tough straight-ahead blocker, similar to an I-formation fullback, because he leads the tailback on our off-tackle play with a running shoulder block. It helps to have a big, strong boy at this position.

Diving Over the Top

One of the best short yardage plays we have in our offense is the fullback wedge. Since this play will be explained in detail in the next chapter, I need mention here only that it calls for three interior linemen to power one defensive man straight backward, with everyone else sealing in to his inside. The fullback takes a soft lob center and drives up into the line behind the apex of the wedge.

When going 2 yards or less for a vital first down or touchdown, he will usually dive over the top, keeping his body parallel to the ground. We want him to drive forward until he is about to feel contact before he dives. If the fullback uses the correct diving angle, he will present a small target to the defensive team and be extremely hard to stop.

Sometimes we drill our fullbacks in this diving technique during our preseason practice. In this drill we set up a pile of dummies at the end of a sawdust pit and station our fullbacks in a line about 5 yards away. A coach tosses a short lob pass to each fullback in turn

as he starts forward, and the boy runs up to the pile of dummies and takes off into the sawdust pit.

The Half Spin

The fullback half spin series, our 20 series, is highly effective and easy to teach. Assuming right formation, the ball is centered at the right knee of the fullback. As he catches the ball, he takes a 1-foot step with his right foot and swivels his upper body toward the wingback, who arrives behind him at that instant.

If it is a "keep," the fullback does not extend the ball in a fake to the wingback, who must make a strong fake of taking the ball in both hands as he runs by at top speed. If it is a "give," he swivels and hands off the ball to the wingback, who takes it with both hands and runs wide. The fullback will then fake a carry into the line or fake fading to pass. If the fullback keeps the ball, he will run into the line on a trap play or fade a step or two to pass.

If the fullback is not a passer, the tail and full may switch places so the tailback can fade to pass. Several pass patterns with the tail at fullback are diagrammed in Chapter 6.

The Full Spin

During my coaching career, I have periodically used the fullback full spin series, our 30 series. I have kept returning to it every 5 or 10 years because for me it is a thing of beauty. It can also be extremely effective. But it is more difficult to teach than the fullback half spin, especially for high school players.

I have included the full back's full-spin technique here. But it's not wise to try to use the full spin and the half spin series together in any one season. (See Chapter 5 for discussions of both series.)

Though it appears to be one uninterrupted motion, the fullback's full-spin maneuver can be broken down into three steps. Assuming the spin will be to the left, or counterclockwise, the ball is centered at the left knee of the fullback, who catches it while taking a short position step with his left foot, pointing the toes of that foot almost at the sideline. Then he takes a longer diagonal step of about 12 inches with his right foot and pivots on the ball of that foot. Finally, he finishes with a third step of about 12 inches toward the line. By that time the fullback will be running forward under control whether he has handed off or kept the ball.

The spin maneuver may be compared to the motion of a top, which spins counterclockwise while gaining ground forward. The secret is to teach an inexperienced fullback to step and pivot in easy stages without a football before making him handle the ball.

This series involves the full, the tail, and the wing. The full may give to the tail, or he may fake to the tail and give to the wing, or he may fake to one or both backs and carry the ball himself.

Tailback Techniques

The tailback is always one of the key men in our single wing offense. As mentioned previously, we expect him to have some ability as both a runner and a passer, though we do not expect him to be outstanding at both skills. In addition, even if he is not a good punter when kicking from regular punt formation, we often can teach him to quick-kick reasonably well. He is always one of our better athletes.

There is one important drill I will discuss here that is also mentioned in my passing chapter. We hope both our tailbacks and wingbacks will be able to throw on the move, whether they're running to their left or to their right. It's a matter of flexibility in the upper body, which they can develop in the "across the field" drill used regularly at the beginning of practice: Two boys run back and forth across the field 10 yards apart, throwing and catch-

ing the ball. This has been an invaluable drill for both our tailbacks and wingbacks.

The important details of passing and quick-kicking in the single wing are covered in later chapters of this book. Players can not only be taught the basics of these skills, but can also develop them to a considerable degree.

Developing the running ability of a back in the limited practice time available is a different matter. Little can be done with drills as such to teach a tailback how to become an exceptional ball carrier. In the final analysis, his speed and natural running style will be the determining factors in success. However, you can and should make sure he understands clearly the design of the various plays in your offense.

The drills we use for training this position simulate the actual situations that occur when the plays of our offense are used in games. For example, we drill a tailback on when to keep the ball and when to throw it on our optional running pass by having a defensive man stay back or come up to force the play.

We drill him on running hard on the off-tackle play by having him lower his shoulders and drive through two men positioned close together who slam him with dummies as he passes between them. We drill him on when to run for the corner and when to cut inside on our power-end run by having him key a defensive man's reactions. This type of drill is the only way we can prepare a tailback to cope with the various situations that may arise on the plays in which he assumes a key role.

Running Drills for All Backs

From the strip, all of our backs are drilled on taking the ball and running to their assigned destinations on various plays. This is especially important for the tailback and fullback, who must learn to catch the ball from the center effortlessly before doing anything else. Sometimes as they hit the hole, running

WINNING SINGLE WING FOOTBALL

hard, teammates on either side slam them with light dummies. The tailback does this on the off-tackle play and the end run. The fullback does this on seam bucks and trap plays, and the wingback does this on reverses. We call this our "slam" drill. Of equal importance is our "gauntlet" drill. Each ball carrier runs between two lines of his teammates, who try hard to knock the ball loose from his grasp. This drill teaches the ball carrier to cup his hand over the end of the ball securely in normal running and sometimes to cover up with both hands. It also reminds all of our players of the importance of turnovers. Both of these drills are run with plenty of noise and enthusiasm. They are crucial to our success.

Conclusion

I hope the drills and techniques covered here will be helpful to other single wing coaches. If a coach gets one good idea from a clinic or a book, it is time well spent.

Like any other style of offense, our single wing attack can be effective only when individual players execute the fundamentals of football correctly. No matter how good a play looks on paper, it will not be successful without sharp blocking, sure ball handling, hard running, and coordinated team play. Certain basic techniques must be mastered in each of these areas.

In this chapter I have discussed some of the drills we have found most helpful in teaching the individual techniques used by our players in a game. We utilize each drill for a purpose, and we try to make that purpose clear to the players involved. There is just not time enough to use drills that are not functional in nature.

Chapter 4

STRAIGHT SERIES RUNNING PLAYS

At different places in this book, I discuss the effectiveness of our indirect attack, our passing game, and our formation variations, but the backbone of our offense will always be straight series running plays. If we can't move the ball with such basic plays as the off-tackle, the end run, and fullback bucks, we will be in trouble.

Over the course of my coaching career, I have reduced the number of our straight series running plays. I used to have two off-tackle plays, two end runs, two inside reverses, and two outside reverses. But for years one of each of these plays has been enough for a highly

effective attack. In this chapter I will discuss these four key plays and others in the straight series.

The Off-Tackle (Play No. 48)

We use our off-tackle play (Play No. 48) any place on the field, not only in short yardage. It has been highly effective. (See Figures 28 and 29.) We call the play "48" because there is a 4 center to the tailback, and the play ends up in the area of the No. 8 end.

As he does on all plays in our offense, the No. 8 end calls "Even," if there is a man head-

OFF-TACKLE (PLAY NO. 48)

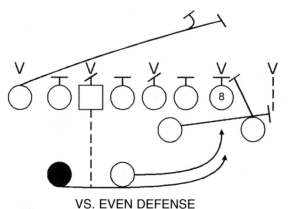

Figure 28   VS. EVEN DEFENSE

OFF-TACKLE (PLAY NO. 48)

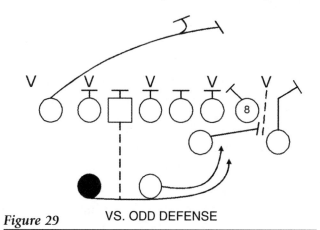

Figure 29   VS. ODD DEFENSE

35

on him or "Odd, " if there is no man head-on him. Our players have blocking rules for each play, and these rules govern all blocking assignments, but the "Even" and "Odd" calls are a help to the players on the strongside of the formation in getting oriented to the defense.

From "far" position (behind the No. 3 lineman), the tailback takes a 4 center, runs an arc, and hits the hole going downfield. Running hard, he aims for the power side of the hole, the side of the double team. He closely follows the blocking fullback. The fullback must also run an arc so that he hits the hole going downfield. He will use a running shoulder block in leading the tailback.

The blocking back lines up closer to the line of scrimmage, as he does on all plays when he does the trapping. He traps the first man beyond the No. 8 end with his head on the inside. In essence, he traps the first man past the double team block.

If there is an "Even" call, the wingback powers the man on No. 8. If there is an "Odd" call, the No. 8 end powers the man on No. 7. On any "Odd" call, the wing influences and blocks to the outside. His influence, a quick fake of a block on the defensive man, sets up the blocking back's trap.

Against a gap defense, the No. 8 end calls "Odd" because there is no man head-on him. All strongside linemen must block their inside seam. There can be no penetration on this all-important play.

Assignments for Play No. 48 Summarized

No. 8   No man on (Odd): Power Man on No. 7.
       Man on (Even): Post for wing.
       Man in inside gap (Odd): Power him.

No. 7   Man on (Odd): Post for No. 8.
       Man on (Even): Block man alone.
       No man on (Even): Step up and protect area.
       Man in inside gap: Block him.

No. 6   Man on: Block him.
       No man on: Step up and protect area.
       Man in inside gap: Block him.

No. 5   Block man from head-on to head-on center.

No. 4   Block man from head-on to weakside.

No. 3   Block man from head-on to weakside.

No. 2   Sprint across shallow to block safety.

Wing   No man on (Even): Power man on No. 8.
       Man on (Odd): Influence, block to outside.

B. Back   Line up closer. Trap first man past No. 8.

Full   Run an arc, leading tailback into hole.

Tail   Take lead center and run an arc into hole.

The End Run (Play No. 49)

One of the strongest plays in the single wing arsenal is the end run. Especially when opponents try to shut off the inside attack, this play is a potential long-gainer. We call this play "49" because there is a 4 center to the tailback and the play ends up in the wide outside zone on the strongside, which we designate 9.

At Wabash College in 1965, when we were twelfth among all the colleges in the country in average yards gained rushing a game, Play No. 49 was by far our most effective running play. It averaged over 9 yards a try and gave us many long runs. In the years since it has remained highly effective.

The details of the end run are not complicated, but executing the play effectively takes a lot of work. I have diagramed the play against different defenses. (See Figures 30 and 31.)

From "near" position (behind the center), the tailback takes a 4 center and runs outside, sizing up the reactions of the opponent's force man, the end man on the line of scrimmage.

END RUN (PLAY NO. 49)

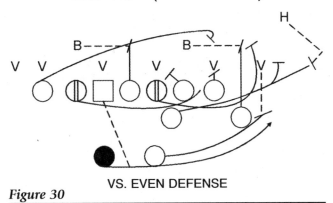

VS. EVEN DEFENSE

Figure 30

END RUN (PLAY NO. 49)

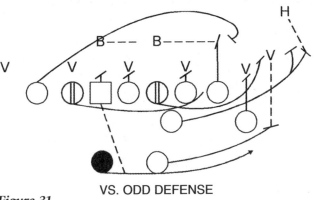

VS. ODD DEFENSE

Figure 31

The fullback will block that man, but he must adjust to the movement of the defensive man as the play develops. If the force man runs straight upfield, determined to contain the end run, the fullback will knock him out with a shoulder block and the tailback will cut inside the block and out again. Under current high school rules the full may not block him below the waist.

If the end man on the line plays passively, the full will turn downfield to block him. The most difficult defensive man to play against is one who comes across hard at about 45 degrees to meet the full head-on, making a pile. The tail may still avoid the pile and continue outside, but this may hurt the timing of the play. A good blocking fullback can really help you here.

The blocking back lines up a bit deeper and sprints through the wing's original area as a personal interferer. When he clears that area, he may take different actions, depending on the reaction of the defense. If the halfback comes up quickly outside, the blocking back will knock him out and the tail will cut inside his block. If the half comes up more slowly, he will block him deeper in the secondary.

Especially in a short-yardage or goal-line situation, we may encounter a "bunched defense," in which our opponents are expecting an inside play. In this case, the blocking back will turn to the inside to block as quickly as possible, with the full continuing to lead the tail outside.

The wingback will block anyone on any part of him to inside gap. Otherwise he takes the first backer head-up to inside. He will often get help from the pulling No. 6 lineman.

There is one other key point on this play. No. 6 must not pull against a packed defense. A packed defense has a lineman on No. 7 and a lineman or a moved-up backer on No. 6. If it's this sort of defense, No. 7 could not block the man on him and also fill for a pull by No. 6. So instead of pulling, No. 6 blocks the man on him, and this would include a backer who's ready to blitz. No. 6 decides on his own whether to pull or not. No call is necessary.

Assignments for Play No. 49 Summarized

No. 8   Man on (Even): Block him.
         No man on (Odd): Block backer head-up to inside.

No. 7   Block man from outside seam to head-on No. 6.

No. 6   Shallow-pull around end and look to inside.
         Don't pull versus packed defenses. If packed, block man head-on.

No. 5   Man on: Block him. No man on: Block backer.

No. 4   Block man from head-on to head-on No. 3.

No. 3   Pull over No. 7 seam and seal.

No. 2   Sprint across shallow to peel.

Tail   Take lead and run end run.

Full   Block end man on line.

B. Back Run through wing's original area to block downfield.

Wing   Block any man on any part of you to inside gap.

Otherwise block first backer head-up to inside.

INSIDE REVERSE (PLAY NO. 43)

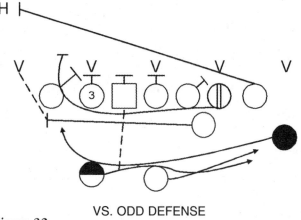

VS. ODD DEFENSE

Figure 32

INSIDE REVERSE (PLAY NO. 43)

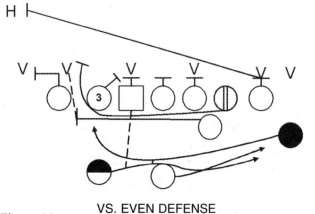

VS. EVEN DEFENSE

Figure 33

The Inside Reverse (Play No. 43)

The simplified inside reverse we use has been highly effective. (See Figures 32 and 33.) We designate the play this way because there is a 4 center to the tailback and the play ends up in the area of the No. 3 lineman.

On this play the tailback and fullback should align 2 or 3 feet closer to the line of scrimmage. Also the wingback should line up slightly deeper than usual. This shading helps the wing get back to take the handoff from the tailback. The wing's depth is not a giveaway because he will line up this way on some other plays.

From "far" position the tail takes a 4 center and carries the ball over to hand it forward to the wing. After the handoff, the tail fakes the Keep Play. The wing takes the ball and carries into the 3 hole. He must run downfield, following the pulling No. 7. The full fakes the Keep. Lining up closer to the line, the blocking back traps the first man past the No. 3 lineman.

The No. 8 end elbows the man on No. 7 or on himself as he sprints across shallow to knock the far halfback to the outside. No. 7 makes a shallow pull through the hole to block the backer. No. 6 checks the man on him or the first man to his outside. The No. 5 lineman blocks any man on him or steps forward to prevent any penetration. The center posts any man on him or (no man on him) steps forward to prevent penetration.

The No. 3 powers any man from his inside gap to head-on the center. His first priority is to block that inside gap. If there is a man on him or on his outside shoulder, No. 3 posts him. The No. 2 end has a key role. If there is a defensive man on him or on his inside shoulder, he influences and checks the next man outside. Otherwise he powers the first man on or off the line to the inside.

Assignments for Play No. 43 Summarized

No. 8   Elbow man on No. 7 or man on you, and sprint over to block far halfback to the outside.

No. 7   Shallow-pull through hole to block backer.

No. 6   Check man on or first man to your outside.

No. 5   Block man on or (no man on) step forward to brace up.

No. 4   Man on: Post. No man on: Step forward to brace up.

No. 3   Power man from inside gap to head-on center.
Man on or man on outside shoulder: Post.

No. 2   Man on or inside shoulder: Influence and check next man outside.
Otherwise power first man on or off the line to the inside.

Tail   Hand ball forward to wing and fake Keep.

Full   Run to strongside and fake Keep.

B. Back Line up closer. Trap first man past No. 3.

Wing   Take handoff from tail and run through hole.

The Keep Play

This would be a good time to discuss the Keep Play, a highly effective check on Play No. 43. These two plays look similar to the defense. On both plays the No. 7 pulls to the weakside, the blocking back and the wingback run to the weakside, and the tail hands off or fakes handing off to the wing before running to the strongside behind the blocking fullback. On this play the tail fakes handing to the wing and keeps the ball. Thus the name "Keep." Both

KEEP PLAY

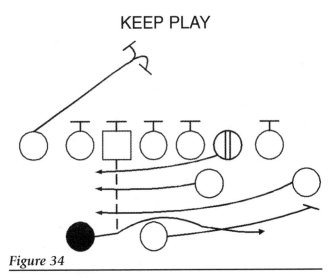

Figure 34

backs must do a realistic job of faking the handoff. Figure 34 shows the Keep Play.

The Keep is a play single wing coaches have used successfully for many years, but you can't just call it at any time. It should be set up by the successful use of Play No. 43. It has worked best with the formation (whether right or left) set into the narrow side of the field because the defensive players think first of defending the wide side.

On the Keep Play many coaches have pulled the No. 8 end instead of the No. 7 because the No. 8 is closer to the defensive end and can possibly exert a greater influence on him. I used to do this, but in recent years I have pulled No. 7 for two reasons: there is less new to teach and I can now have the Keep Pass Play also with no change in line assignments. Pulling No. 7 works very well. (See Chapter 6 for the Keep Pass Play.) I have included both the Keep and the Keep Pass Play in my discussion of blocking-back false key plays in Chapter 10 on aspects of single wing strategy.

Play No. 23 Quick

As I pointed out in Chapter 2, we can use 3-hole blocking with a number of different backfield cycles. One of the simplest and most effective of these maneuvers is Play No. 23 Quick. (See Figure 35.) There is no change of

PLAY NO. 23 QUICK

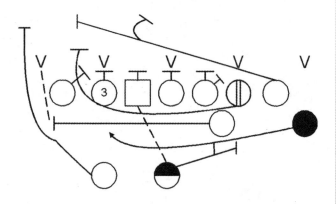

VS. ODD DEFENSE

Figure 35

OUTSIDE REVERSE (PLAY NO. 21 POWER)

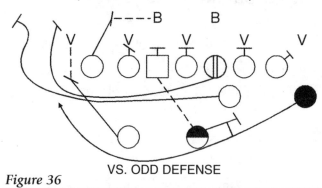

VS. ODD DEFENSE

Figure 36

OUTSIDE REVERSE (PLAY NO. 21 POWER)

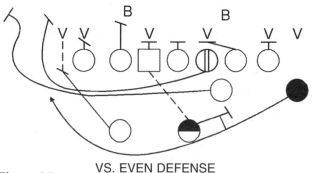

VS. EVEN DEFENSE

Figure 37

assignments from Play No. 43 for any lineman or the blocking back, though the other backfield men run a different play. From far position the tailback fakes an outside block on the end and runs down to block the halfback. The fullback takes a 2 center and steps up and over to hand the ball forward to the wingback, who carries through the hole.

The Outside Reverse (Play No. 21 Power)

This play is an old single wing favorite that has always been effective. In earlier years we had two or three strongside linemen pulling in front of the ball carrier. Now, for the sake of simplicity and greater speed, we pull only No. 6. But however you block it, this is a play that belongs in the attack of every single wing team.

We call this play "21 Power" because there is a 2 center and the play ends up in the wide outside zone on the weakside, which we designate as 1. Figures 36 and 37 show Play No. 21 Power run against odd and even defenses.

From far position the tailback runs up to block the weakside defensive end, aiming at a spot slightly outside his target. He must not loop to get outside position or the end may dart inside him and disrupt the play. The full takes a 2 center, hands off behind him to the wing, and picks off any pursuit.

Unless we have a big, rugged tailback, we often have the tail and full switch places so the full blocks the end, a job he's used to doing. Then we call the play "Zip 21 Power." This switch has not been a giveaway because from Zip we can run a strong off-tackle play with the full carrying, an inside trap with the tail carrying, or any number of other plays. I will discuss the use of such checks in Chapter 10 on single wing strategy. The blocking back lines up deeper and sprints around end to block the defensive halfback. He anticipates that the halfback will usually come up wide so he will block him to the outside and the wing will cut inside the block. The wing starts a count early as part of the 20 series, but if you are not using the 20 series, you may not want to start him in quick motion.

Now for the linemen's assignments: The No. 6 lineman pulls around end to block downfield. If necessary, the No. 7 must fill for No. 6's pull. His rule is to block any man from on No. 6 to on himself. The No. 8 end will normally block any man on him or first man outside. However, against a packed defense (defensive men on both No. 6 and No. 7), No. 7 calls for help, and both he and No. 8 block to their inside. The fullback must be alert to pick off any chaser.

The No. 5 lineman blocks any man on him or, if uncovered, braces up to protect his area. The center's rule is exactly like the No. 5's. The No. 3 lineman and the No. 2 end have the same blocking rule: They block any man from inside gap to head-on. Otherwise they block the first backer head-up to inside.

Assignments for Play No. 21 Power Summarized

No. 8   Block man on or first man outside. If packed defense, block to inside.

No. 7   Block man on No. 6 to man on you.

No. 6   Pull around end to block downfield.

No. 5   Block man on you or (no man on) brace up.

No. 4   Block man on you or (no man on) brace up.

No. 3   Man inside gap to head-on: Block him. Otherwise block first backer head-up to inside.

No. 2   Man inside gap to head-on: Block him. Otherwise block first backer head-up to inside.

Tail   Block end man on line.

Full   Hand off behind to wing and pick off pursuit.

B. Back   Line up deeper. Sprint around end to block outside.

Wing   Take ball from full and carry around end.

Fullback Seam Bucks

Fullback seam bucks are an important part of our attack. On these quick-hitting power plays the fullback takes the snap and follows the blocking back into the hole. From their upright stance, both the fullback and the blocking back must take a short backward false step to get started going forward. Otherwise they will be leaning before the snap and pick up a motion penalty.

These plays get their name from the way two adjacent linemen open a seam between them. The first digit is a 1, indicating there will be a soft lob center to the fullback. The second digit designates the seam through which the blocking back and fullback will run. For example, if the play number is 16, the seam

SEAM BUCK (PLAY NO. 16)

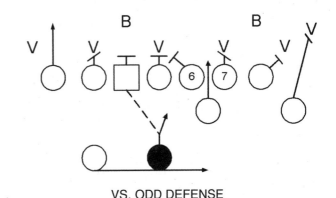

VS. ODD DEFENSE

Figure 38

SEAM BUCK (PLAY NO. 16)

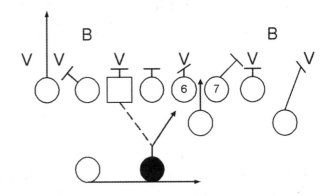

VS. EVEN DEFENSE

Figure 39

41

will be between No. 6 and No. 7, the next man toward the strongside. If the play number is 15, the full will hit between No. 5 and No. 6. If the play number is 17, he will hit between No. 7 and No. 8. If the play number is 13, he will hit between No. 3 and No. 4.

Play Nos. 16, 15, 17, 13

Figures 38 and 39 show Play No. 16 against different defenses. Figures 40, 41, and 42 show Play Nos. 15, 17, and 13 used versus typical alignments we normally encounter.

The designated lineman and his adjacent teammate should line up with an extra foot of space between them. That will make for a larger opening as they block to the outside. These two players will always block to the outside, even if there is a defensive man (usually a linebacker) squarely in the seam between them. In that case the blocking back will block that man and the fullback will cut off his block.

All the other players have only one rule: to make themselves most useful to the play. They know where the designated opening is, and they see defensive men in position to be blocked. From their position they can see whether a lineman, a linebacker, or a halfback has the most chance of getting to the ball carrier, and they make themselves most useful by blocking the most dangerous man.

These seam bucks are an excellent complement to our outside plays and our traps. More importantly, they are useful to take advantage of an obvious opening in the defensive alignment. They are short yardage plays on which we do not expect many long gains, but we do expect consistent short gains.

Since that is our expectation, I long ago gave up on checking off to a play with a more obvious opening. If suddenly some defensive man moves squarely in the hole, a good performance by the blocking back and the fullback can still allow us to make a short gain.

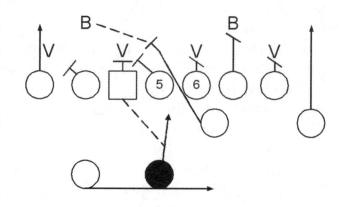

SEAM BUCK (PLAY NO. 15)

VS. EVEN DEFENSE

Figure 40

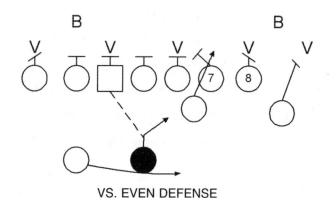

SEAM BUCK (PLAY NO. 17)

VS. EVEN DEFENSE

Figure 41

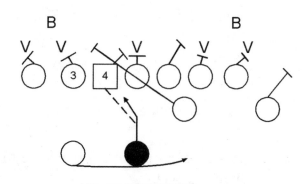

SEAM BUCK (PLAY NO. 13)

VS. ODD DEFENSE

Figure 42

Special Plays with "Seam Buck" Blocking

Closely akin to our seam bucks are plays in which the tailback carries the ball with "seam buck" blocking. These are important because each one adds a new dimension to the attack. We use 5 as the first digit to designate these plays.

TAILBACK SEAM BUCK (PLAY NO. 57)

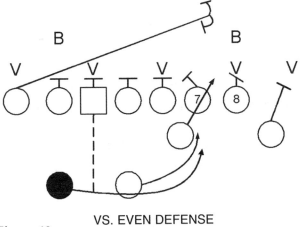

VS. EVEN DEFENSE

Figure 43

Play No. 57 (Tailback Seam Buck)

The first of these is Play No. 57, which uses 17 blocking. (See Figure 43.) From far position the tailback takes a lead center and runs an arc, following the fullback into the seam between No. 7 and No. 8. The assignments for the linemen are exactly like Play No. 17. The blocking back goes through the hole before the fullback, giving us a powerful off-tackle play with two backs in front of the ball carrier.

Play No. 57 X

An extremely effective variation of this maneuver is Play No. 57 X, on which the blocking back runs to the weakside as a false key with the No. 8 and No. 7 cross-blocking to open the hole. (I discuss the use of false keys in Chapter 10.) When cross-blocking, No. 8 goes first and No. 7 crosses behind him. If the next inside man is too far away for No. 8 to reach, he and No. 7 block as they do on regu-

TAILBACK SEAM BUCK (PLAY NO. 57 X)

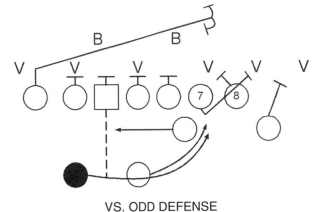

VS. ODD DEFENSE

Figure 44

lar 57. There is no change of assignment for any other player. (See Figure 44.)

TAILBACK SEAM BUCK (PLAY NO. 56)

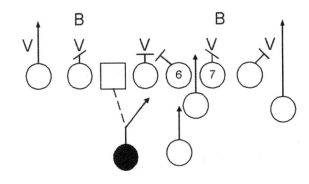

VS. ODD DEFENSE

Figure 45

Play No. 56 (Tailback Seam Buck)

Play No. 56 uses 16 blocking. We have implemented it at times with success. From close position (left foot on the ball in right formation), the tailback takes a 1 center and follows both the blocking back and the fullback into the seam between No. 6 and No. 7. This play can be especially effective against the kind of defense shown here. The blocking back blocks the first backer, and the fullback looks to the inside for the weakside backer. (See Figure 45.) In a Lawrenceville School game in 1967 we used this as our main play to make a number of first downs in a row on an important drive.

SEAM BUCK (PLAY NO. 12)

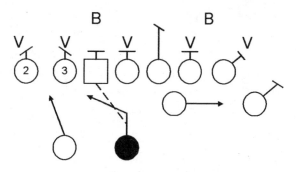

VS. ODD DEFENSE

Figure 46

Play No. 12

Next I will discuss Play No 12, which has been highly effective for us. (See Figure 46.) With the tailback in far position, the fullback takes a 1 center and makes a good inside fake before running over into an opening formed by No. 2 and No. 3. The tailback goes straight ahead under control, expecting to go through the opening and block a backer. But if the defense is massed inside in short yardage situations, the No. 2 end may block to his inside and the tailback and fullback skid to the outside. All linemen follow the normal seam-buck procedure of blocking the most dangerous man. The blocking back runs to the strongside as a false key. In recent years we have used Play No. 12 more than any other seam buck.

The Fullback Wedge

The most dependable short yardage play we have is the fullback wedge. (See Figures 47 and 48.) On this play we form an apex with two or three linemen to drive one defensive man straight backward, with everyone else sealing to his inside.

Either No. 5 or No. 6, whoever has a defensive man playing on him, forms the apex of the wedge. He aims his helmet directly at the man in front of him and drives. The apex man will have help from a teammate on ei-

ther side of him. All other linemen and the wingback seal to the inside. We emphasize that these players block space, not men.

In the beginning, this type of blocking is hard to get across because players naturally want to help out by blocking individual men. And it's hard to teach this blocking unless you do it live. The same problem exists in training the blocking back on his assignment, which is filling the space between the No. 5 and the center. This is crucial because the center cannot make an accurate pass to the fullback and still start as quickly as the other linemen. The blocking back must go through the No. 5's *original* area to fill that space before the center gets going. He must learn to do this under live conditions.

The fullback takes a soft lob center and runs forward, aiming for the seam between No. 5 and No. 6. At the goal line he will usually dive

FULLBACK WEDGE

(#6 IS APEX)

VS. EVEN DEFENSE

Figure 47

FULLBACK WEDGE

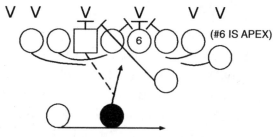

(#5 IS APEX)

VS. ODD DEFENSE

Figure 48

over the top for a score, following the technique outlined in Chapter 3. Elsewhere on the field he may sometimes go over the top for a first down, but usually he just drives hard, trying to pick up yardage. From far position the tailback usually fakes an end run, although I'm not sure this fake does any good.

The blocking rules for the No. 5 and No. 6 linemen are simply stated. If either player has a defensive man on him, he will consider himself the apex of the wedge and drive forward into his opponent. If there is a man lined up in the seam between them, they will drive that man back together. If there are defensive men on both No. 5 and No. 6, they will drive forward in unison, with their teammates sealing to the inside as usual. Naturally all linemen will cut down their line splits to a minimum beforehand.

Although the assignments for this play are simple, it takes a great deal of repetition to develop a good wedge charge. The play must be practiced live, and we have always been reluctant to use it too many times in our own scrimmages. It's tough on the boy lining up opposite No. 5 or No. 6.

Over the years this play has been highly consistent. Our players have been confident they can make a critical yard, regardless of the defensive alignment. Statistics will bear this out. From 1991 to 1996 we ran the wedge many times in short yardage, and only once, in a game in 1992, did we fail to make a first down or a touchdown. That failure occurred when our fullback ran wide toward the area of the No. 8 end instead of running straight ahead behind the apex of the wedge. If you have to make a critical yard, the fullback wedge is a good bet.

Solo Play

The last running play I will discuss here is what we call "Solo." Over the years it has some-

SOLO PLAY

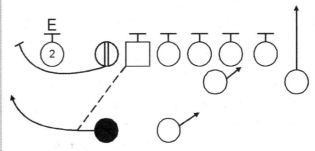

Figure 49

times been referred to as the "Tailback Sneak" or "Tailback Naked." (See Figure 49.)

From far position and lined up deeper, the tailback takes a lead center to the weakside and runs around that end. The play depends upon surprise. In our offense we usually don't attack the weakside without some element of delay. We often run reverses, but these all have some initial fake to the strongside or up the middle. If once or twice a game we run directly to the weakside with our best back carrying the ball, it can be highly effective.

The other details of this play can be covered easily. We ask the No. 2 end to split out about 4 feet in hopes that the defensive end will play head-up on him. The No. 2 blocks that end, wherever he lines up, keeping contact as long as possible. If the defensive man widens so our end has to push him out, the tail should cut inside him.

The center's job is not easy. He must lead the tailback to the weakside, and to do it he may have to set his feet and body slightly in that direction beforehand. Obviously this center pass takes extra practice.

Using a strongside variation, such as splitting out the No. 8 end or the wingback, may increase the possibility of surprise on this play. But with or without such a variation, the defensive end is often caught flat-footed by an unexpected run to the weakside.

Although we have used it sparingly, Solo has given us a number of big gains at crucial times. If I were still coaching, I would use it more often than I did. In a game in 1994, with a fast runner at tailback, we used it three times: from right formation for gains of 13 yards and 39 yards (and a touchdown), and from left formation for 30 yards. Solo is a play that should be in the repertoire of every single wing team.

Conclusion

The straight series running plays discussed in this chapter are essential to the success of our single wing offense. If we cannot establish such basic plays as the end run, the off-tackle, the inside reverse, and fullback bucks, almost certainly we will not be successful with the passes and the more deceptive plays in our offense.

Chapter 5

INDIRECT ATTACK PLAYS

One of the strongest parts of our offense is the indirect attack. The delayed and deceptive cycles used in this portion of our offense effectively blend the power blocking and the trap blocking that is characteristic of the single wing running attack.

These delayed-cycle plays, in contrast to straight-hitting plays, are somewhat similar to change-of-pace pitches in baseball. Good pitchers vary the speed of their pitches. I go back here to the statement made by Coach Jordan Olivar in his letter quoted in the Preface that *the timing of the single wing is so different from the T formation boys continually face that the defense just gets out of position enough and is unable to react the way they do to the T.*

In this chapter I will discuss these delayed cycles, showing how they work and listing some of their strengths. At the end of this discussion I will suggest ways in which these indirect attack plays may be used with a minimum amount of teaching.

Cycles Used in the Indirect Attack

When coaches talk of a cycle or a series, they are referring to a group of plays that look alike in their origin but end up attacking different areas of the defense. Over the years the most popular of the indirect cycles used by single wing teams have been the full spin of the fullback spinning to the tailback and often to the wingback as well (our 30 series), the fullback half spin to the wingback (our 20 series), the tailback half spin to the fullback (our 80 series), and the buck lateral series, in which the fullback carries the ball forward to fake or give to the blocking back, who has pivoted around with his back to the line on the starting count.

Although I played on a team that utilized the buck lateral series with great success, as a coach I have only dabbled with it from time to time and never really used it. In this book I am discussing only those plays and maneuvers we have coached and utilized. We have used the other three series successfully for many years.

I should say something here about why we have not used the buck lateral series. Much of the strength of that series depends upon having a smooth ball handler and good passer at blocking back. Especially at the high school level, I do not think it's reasonable to expect a boy to have those abilities and be the kind of blocker we need for our single wing attack.

Furthermore, we often encounter the Oklahoma Defense adjusted, with the strong safety up on the strongside. This defensive alignment stymies the two best plays of the buck lateral cycle, the pitchout to the tailback and the trap by the No. 3 lineman with the fullback carrying. Most importantly, from the buck lateral series it is impossible to use the 4-hole trap, our most consistent indirect attack play.

The 4-Hole Trap

From any of the three series mentioned above, the best play is the 4-hole trap. The blocking for the line and the blocking back is identical on 24, 34, and 84, the three plays I'll discuss that use this trap play.

As with other trap plays from the indirect attack, the type of backfield action and faking we use is designed to pull certain defensive players out of position or at least to freeze them so assigned blockers can get to them. On any 4-hole play we block the backers to the outside, and the ball carrier often seems to appear in the secondary from nowhere.

On a 4-hole trap, if you have a fast and shifty ball carrier, he often needs only one fake in the secondary to go for a long gain. One of the best examples I can remember came in the fourth quarter of a close game at Lawrenceville School in 1973 when on play No. 84 our tailback ran for the winning touchdown. He darted into the secondary, cut sharply to his left, and ran for 74 yards.

Play No. 24 and 4-Hole Blocking

Let's start a detailed discussion of the 4-hole trap with Play No. 24. (See Figures 50 and 51.) From far position (behind the No. 3 lineman) the tailback runs hard toward the weakside and fakes a block on the end from the outside before running downfield to block

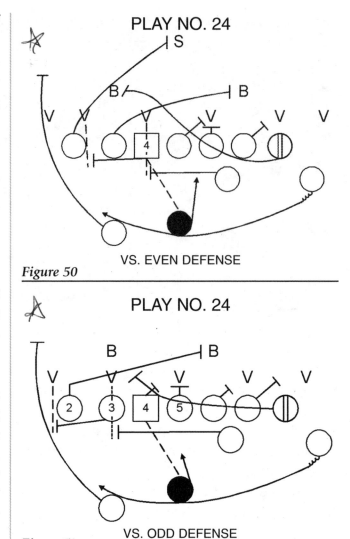

PLAY NO. 24

VS. EVEN DEFENSE

Figure 50

PLAY NO. 24

VS. ODD DEFENSE

Figure 51

the halfback. Assuming right formation, the ball is centered at the right knee of the fullback (a 2 center). As he catches the ball, the full takes about a 1-foot step with his right foot and swivels his upper body toward the wingback, who arrives behind him at that instant. The full does not extend the ball to the wing, but lets the wing do the faking, as he keeps the ball and runs low and hard into the line.

The wingback starts a count early and times it so he arrives behind the full at exactly the right instant. The wing fakes taking the ball with both hands and snaps his hands to his left hip as he runs at top speed to the outside. The blocking back aligns closer to the line of scrimmage and traps the first man on or past the No. 4 man, the center.

The No. 8 end makes a shallow pull past the power block and across the line to block the far backer. No. 8 does not make a pull in the usual sense. Assuming right formation, he takes a step to the inside with his left foot as the No. 7 takes a step with his right foot forward and to the outside. No. 7's job is to check the first lineman on or past the No. 8 end. The No. 8 end runs through the area where the feet of No. 7 and No. 6 were originally. These players have moved forward on the snap.

Now for other line assignments: The No. 6 posts any man on him or, if there's no man on him, he blocks the first lineman to his outside. The No. 5 posts a man on him or, if there's no man on him, powers the man on No. 6. The center influences a man on him and checks the weakside tackle. In other words, he gets out of the way as quickly as possible. (Defensive linemen love to charge into the center and are usually vulnerable to a trap.) If there's no man on him, the center powers the man on No. 5.

Regardless of the rest of the defense, with no man on him, the No. 3 lineman crosses over to block the strongside backer. If there is a man on him, the No. 3 says "You" to the No. 2 end and influences that man on him as he pulls to the outside to block the end. The "You" call is a signal to the No. 2 end, "You take my block."

If we are using a number of 4-hole plays, the No. 3 should make some dummy "You" calls on plays that end up elsewhere. The No. 2 end blocks the safety unless he gets a "You" call from No. 3. If he does get that call, he blocks the far backer. A coach can naturally use any word he desires for that "You" call. I am describing our plays exactly as we have run them.

4-Hole Line Assignments Summarized

No. 8   Shallow-pull to block first backer past the hole.

No. 7   Block first lineman on or past No. 8 end.

No. 6   Man on: Post for No. 5.
No Man on: Block first lineman to outside.

No. 5   Man on: Post. No man on: Power.

No. 4   Man on: Influence and block first man to weakside.
No man on: Power man on No. 5.

No. 3   No man on: Block first backer past the hole.
Man on: "You" call to No. 2. Influence and block weakside end.

No. 2   "You" call from No. 3: Block first backer past the hole. Otherwise block safety.

4-Hole Plays Have Been Consistent

The 4-hole play has been consistently successful for many years with both my small college and schoolboy teams. We have used Play No. 24 as often as eight times in a high school game. In a Lawrenceville School game in 1993, against a physically superior team, we used Play No. 24 seven times for a total of 65 yards. There was nothing extraordinary here: no plays that failed to gain yardage and the longest gain was 18 yards, but a number of first downs that kept drives going, helping us win a big game.

Play No. 34 and Play No. 84 have been equally consistent: steady gains and sometimes a long run. Whether the play is 24, 34, or 84, the blocking for all linemen and the blocking back is the same.

PLAY NO. 34

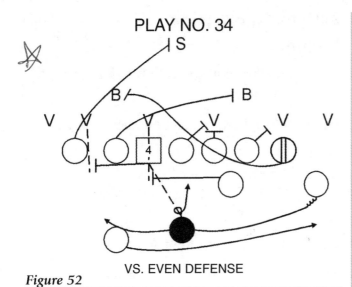

VS. EVEN DEFENSE

Figure 52

Play No. 34

Figure 52 shows Play No. 34. The full takes a 3 center (to his left knee in right formation) and spins to the tail and the wing before hitting the hole. In order to have smooth execution, the full should align in a heel-toe relationship in front of the tail and 1 yard away. On this play the tail must run parallel to the line of scrimmage, allowing room for the wingback to go in front of him. They should both stay low and do the best possible job of faking. It is a thing of beauty to see the fullback come out of his full spin and accelerate through the hole to make good yardage. (See Chapter 3 for a detailed discussion of the full spin.)

PLAY NO. B 84

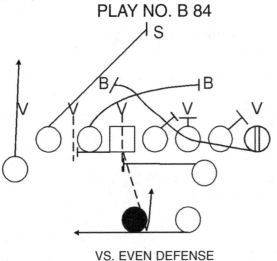

VS. EVEN DEFENSE

Figure 53

Play No. B 84

When we use Play No. 84, we often flank the wingback wide to the strongside (Variation A) or wide or close to the weakside (Variation B). Figure 53 shows Play No. B 84 with the wing flanked close to the weakside. As on all 80 plays, the tailback lines up in close position (left foot on the ball in right formation). This alignment is essential. The tailback takes an 8 center (to his right knee) and half-spins to the faking fullback before running into the hole. The tail's actions on the 80 series are exactly like the full's actions on the 20 series.

ACTION ON 80 PASSES

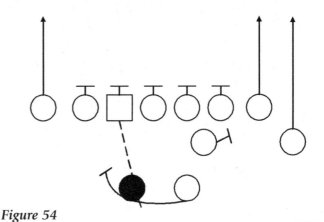

Figure 54

80 Pass Action

This fake maneuver is also executed on 80 passes. Having those 80 passes as part of the cycle is one of the strongest reasons for using this series. On 80 passes all interior linemen and the blocking back execute their usual dropback (Zero) protection assignments. The full fakes taking the ball and then sets up in his usual position for protection as the tail fades to pass. Figure 54 shows this action on 80 passes. This series gives us excellent play-action pass fakes with very little new teaching. I'll discuss 80 passes in detail in the next chapter.

Two Important 30 Series Plays

PLAY NO. 37 (SPIN OFF-TACKLE)

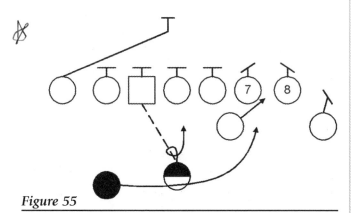

Figure 55

PLAY NO. 35

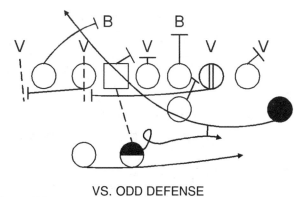

VS. ODD DEFENSE

Figure 56

PLAY NO. 35

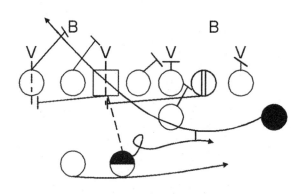

VS. EVEN DEFENSE

Figure 57

Play No. 37

If you are using the 30 series, you will need an off-tackle play to the strongside: Play No. 37. (See Figure 55.) We used to pull two line-men on this play, but it is much easier to use 17 (and 57) blocking as the blocking back leads the tailback through the hole. With the assignments identical for most players on 17, 57, and 37, we are getting "three for the price of one." On Play No. 37 the No. 8 and No. 7 may X block (as on 57 X) if the defense de-mands it.

Like other 30 series plays, the tailback will be in far position and the fullback will align in a heel-toe relationship a yard away from him. The ball is centered at the full's left knee (in right formation) and he spins counter-clockwise, giving the ball to the tail with his left hand before faking into the line, running low and hard. To attain smooth execution, the tail runs through the full's original position, taking the ball with two hands and running an arc into the off-tackle hole. This is an easy way to get a good play with very little new teaching. In the second game of the 1998 Lawrenceville season, our tailback ran for a 57-yard touchdown on this play.

Play No. 35

Play No. 35 is important in this simplified 30 series because it is a consistently successful play and because it has an excellent false key by the blocking back. In 1995 Coach Jim Ahern of Ithaca (M.I.) High School showed me his version of the play, with which he has had tre-mendous success. We have used it and liked it very much. (See Figures 56 and 57.)

Here are the details of this play. From far position the tailback fakes taking the ball from the fullback and runs flat to the strongside. The fullback takes a 3 center and spins counter-clockwise but not as far around as usual. He ends up his spin facing the No. 8 end and immediately steps forward to hand off the ball with his left hand to the wingback, who is making a shallow pull.

The blocking back lines up slightly deeper and shaded over to behind the No. 6 lineman. This is to leave room for the No. 7 lineman's pull. The blocking back runs through the area vacated by the pulling No. 7 and blocks the first defender he encounters. Thus he is a false key. (See Chapter 10 on offensive strategy for a discussion of false key plays.)

The most important assignment in the line is that of the No. 7, who pulls and traps the first man on or past the center. The No. 8 end blocks a man on him or the first man to his outside. The No. 2 end blocks the first backer to his inside. The No. 6 lineman blocks any man on him or (if uncovered) the first backer he encounters.

The blocking at the point of attack is familiar: It's similar to that on 34. The No. 5 blocks any man on him or (if uncovered) he powers the man on No. 6. If there's a man on the center, he influences and traps the first man to the weakside. If there's no man on the center, he powers the man on No. 5. If there's a man on No. 3, he influences and traps the first man to the weakside. If there's no man on him, the No. 3 blocks the backer to the inside or the first defender he encounters.

I have shown this play with the fullback spinning, which is the best way to run it, but I have seen it run successfully with the full taking a 2 center and stepping over quickly to give to the wingback with his left hand as he does on Play No. 23 Quick. In any event, this is a fast-hitting play, one on which the wingback does not attempt to hit the hole running downfield, as he usually does, but slices through the hole at an angle.

Adding the 3 Hole to the Indirect Attack

It is a simple matter to add 3-hole plays to the indirect attack because the assignments for the linemen and the blocking back are identi-

cal with those on Play No. 43. I will diagram these plays against an Oklahoma Defense adjusted. The usual 3-hole blocking rules would apply against other defensive alignments.

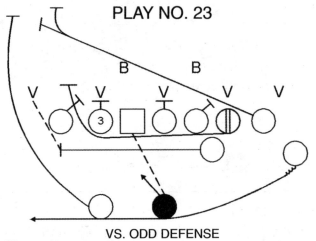

PLAY NO. 23

VS. ODD DEFENSE

Figure 58

Play No. 23

On Play No. 23 the techniques of the backs are the same as on Play No. 24 except that now the blocking back traps the first man past No. 3 and the fullback runs into the 3 hole. (See Figure 58.)

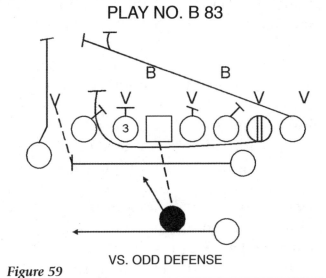

PLAY NO. B 83

VS. ODD DEFENSE

Figure 59

Play No. B 83

On Play No. 83 the assignments for the line and blocking back are like Play No. 23. As on all 80 series plays, the tailback lines up in close position, half-spins to the faking fullback, and runs into the hole. On the 80 series, the wingback is often flanked in different places, depending on what we're doing offensively. I have set him here as a close weakside flanker (Variation B) to threaten the defensive end and widen the hole for the blocking back's trap. (See Figure 59.)

PLAY NO. 33 (SPIN REVERSE)

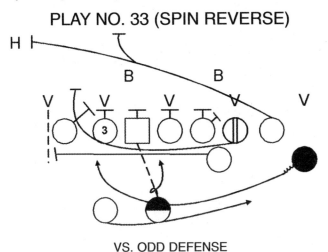

VS. ODD DEFENSE

Figure 60

Play No. 33

On Play No. 33 the full takes a 3 center (to his left knee) and spins counterclockwise, faking to the tail before handing off to the wing with his right hand. (We're assuming right formation.) The tail must run parallel to the line of scrimmage to allow room for the wing to go in front of him. The wing takes the ball and runs downfield into the hole. (See Figure 60.)

Outside Reverses from the Indirect Attack

Play No. 21 Power and Play No. 31 Power

In the previous chapter I discussed Play No. 21 Power. This is the familiar outside reverse from the 20 series, with the tailback blocking the end and the fullback handing off to the wingback, who runs wide to the weakside. Assuming right formation, the full takes a 2 center (at his right knee) and half-spins to give the ball to the wing, who starts a count early. Figure 61 shows 21 Power.

PLAY NO. 21 POWER (OUTSIDE REVERSE)

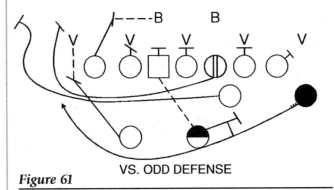

VS. ODD DEFENSE

Figure 61

If you are using the 30 series, you can run the identical play with the fullback taking a 3 center (at his left knee) and making a full spin counterclockwise to give the ball to the wingback with his right hand as he does on 33. The wing starts a count early and runs under control so he can arrive on time for the handoff. The tail blocks the end as on 21 Power. (See Figure 62.)

As I said earlier, it is not wise to include both the 20 series and the 30 series in your attack at the same time. However, for the sake of simplicity, I have lumped these two outside reverse plays together in my discussion here.

PLAY NO. 31 POWER (SPIN OUTSIDE REVERSE)

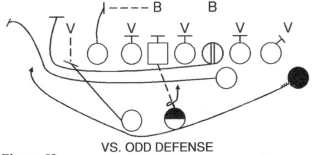

VS. ODD DEFENSE

Figure 62

Play No. 81 and Play No. B 81 Crack

We have two slightly different plays to get outside from the 80 series. In each case the tailback makes the usual half spin to hand off to the fullback, who runs outside. In each case also the assignments for all linemen are iden-

PLAY NO. A 81

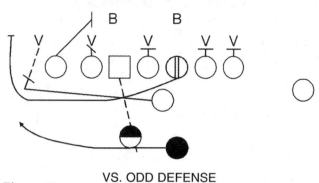

VS. ODD DEFENSE

Figure 63

tical with those on Play No. 21 Power, but on these 80 series plays the ball carrier gets outside more quickly than he does on 21 Power.

Play No. A 81

On Play No. 81 the blocking back blocks the defensive end. Here I show this play with the wing set wide at Variation A, a maneuver designed to move the secondary wider to the strongside. Now we call it "Play No. A 81." (See Figure 63.)

PLAY NO. B 81 CRACK

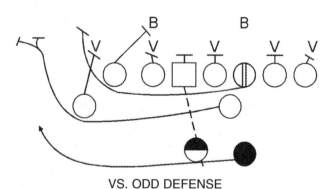

VS. ODD DEFENSE

Figure 64

Play No. B 81 Crack

On Play No. B 81 Crack, the close-flanking wingback is an extra blocker to give us a key block on the weakside defensive end. (See Figure 64.) Sometimes, when using this play, we have had the fullback and wingback change places if it gives us a stronger blocker and a faster ball carrier. Complementary inside plays

to B 81 Crack that work well with a good runner at tailback are B 83 and B 84.

Special Plays in the Indirect Attack

There are a number of special running plays in the indirect attack. I will discuss two of them in detail here. In the next chapter I will discuss pass plays that evolve from the indirect attack.

PLAY NO. 21 DOUBLE REVERSE

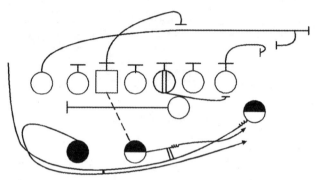

Figure 65

Play No. 21 Double Reverse

The double reverse from the 20 series is a logical extension of that series. We call it "21 Double Reverse."

First of all, a coach must understand what he's trying to do with the play. This is a play that should be used after it has been set up by a number of 20 series plays, which of course all involve certain details: the wingback in quick motion, the half spin of the full giving to the wing, and both the blocking back and the tailback running to the weakside. Now, maybe once a game, the tailback ends up running around the strongside end. Figure 65 shows Play No. 21 Double Reverse.

I should add that when the wing goes in motion, many teams start secondary rotation to the weakside. When this is the case, we have a number of running and passing plays to counter this rotation. Teams that do this are vulnerable to double-reverse action.

This is not a play that is consistent for steady gains, like an off-tackle play. If set up properly, however, it can be a real game-breaker. Over the years we have had a number of long runs with it. In a close game at Lawrenceville School in 1978, our tailback ran the double reverse for a 47-yard touchdown that provided our margin of victory.

Here are the details of Play No. 21 Double Reverse. The wingback goes in quick motion and takes the ball from the fullback as on Play No. 21 Power. The full takes a 2 center and hands off before pausing unobtrusively for several seconds facing the strongside. At the command of "Go" from the tailback, the fullback runs forward to block the end man on the line. He usually blocks that man to the inside, but if the defensive man goes too far upfield, he will block him out while the tailback runs inside him.

The blocking back runs to the weakside as a false key and blocks the first man past the No. 3 lineman. From far position the tailback takes four steps, starting with his left foot, running toward the weakside. On his fourth step, with his right foot, he pivots around in a tight loop and runs behind the wingback to take a handoff. When he has the ball securely in his hands, he yells "Go" to the fullback, who runs to block the strongside end. The No. 8 end blocks any man in his area, steering him to the inside, then circles outside to peel back.

The line assignments are simply stated. All interior linemen brace up to block, but two of them have extra roles: the center, if uncovered, goes forward and loops to peel, and the No. 6 lineman, if uncovered, pulls to the strongside and looks inside. He will usually block the defensive end. The No. 2 end runs across downfield to block the halfback or to peel back. This play is like a punt return in that it's hard to predict how defensive players will react. But the assignments given here have held up well against different defenses.

In addition to perhaps winning a game for you, the double reverse is fun to practice. And, especially with high school boys, that's important. No matter how well planned, a practice can sometimes be tedious, and it's good to have something different like this that can provide excitement.

PLAY NO. 30 END AROUND

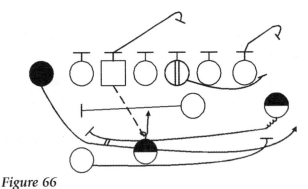

Figure 66

Play No. 30 End Around

Another play we have used that is fun for the players is Play No. 30 End Around. (See Figure 66.) Like Play No. 21 Double Reverse, it must be set up by companion plays. With a fast No. 2 end it has been successful. Again, this is not a consistent play you use frequently. It goes best against a team that is cracking in tight on your strongside and starting rotation in the secondary when the wing goes in motion.

The fullback takes a 3 center and spins counterclockwise, faking to the tailback before handing off to the wingback with his right hand and then faking into the line. So far this backfield action is exactly like Play No. 33. The tailback runs flat as he does on 33 and then goes up to block the end man on the line. The wing carries the ball for a few steps before handing off to the No. 2 end, who has circled deep. Except for the No. 2 end, who is the ball carrier, the line assignments are identical with those on Play No. 21 Double Reverse. The blocking back is again a false key as he runs over to block the first man past the No. 3 lineman.

When used properly, this play has been effective. And I'll guarantee your players will love it, especially the No. 2 end.

Conclusion

In this chapter I have discussed in detail the three cycles in the indirect attack we have used over the years: the 20 series, the 30 series, and the 80 series. I would not advise using all three cycles extensively at one time. However, you do not have to use complete cycles of plays, and you can easily set up a usable mix by adding a couple of 80 series plays to either the 20 series or the 30 series used as your main cycle. That's what I have often done.

If you do this, with little teaching you could easily put in Play No. 84, an 80 pass or two, and (later in the season) perhaps Play No. 81 or Play No. B 81 Crack. You would already have taught the 4-hole assignments, and any 80 pass would use regular dropback (Zero) protection. The assignments for the line on Play Nos. 81 or B 81 Crack would already be taught on Play Nos. 21 Power and 31 Power.

Here's an example of how such a mix might be helpful in getting the most out of your personnel. If you are using the 20 series and your fullback is a mediocre runner, you would not get much yield from Play No. 24. But if you have an outstanding tailback, he should be able to make big gains on Play No. 84.

If the 20 series is your main cycle, you would want at least Play Nos. 24, 21 Power, 21 Pass, and a 20 Pass. You could add Play No. 21 Double Reverse later on. For the simplified 30 series as your main cycle, I would include at least Play Nos. 34, 37, 35, 33, 31 Power, and a 30 Pass. And, remember, all of the above plays except Play Nos. 21 Pass and 21 Power could be used from right formation only. The last two plays should be used from both left and right formation.

No matter how you do it, some form of the indirect attack is essential to a successful single wing offense. These running plays from delayed and deceptive cycles are important, not only because they are good ground-gainers, but also because they offer a change of pace to keep the defense off balance.

In a section of the next chapter I will discuss pass plays that evolve from running plays in the indirect attack. These play-action passes are an important part of the single wing passing game.

Chapter 6

The PASSING GAME

In this chapter I will discuss in detail pass plays we have used that are developed when the basic single wing formation is intact. This is only part of the story because many of our best passes are thrown from strongside or weakside variations of the formation. I will discuss these "variation" passes in Chapter 8.

After brief comments on passing from the single wing and on developing the young passer, I will cover the following pass categories: dropback passes, running passes, running pass variations, reverse passes, play-action passes, special passes, and fake passes. I will show how these different types of passes fit into the total single wing offense.

Some Thoughts on Passing from the Single Wing

Despite what some people think, the single wing is an excellent passing formation. The statistics bear this out. As I said earlier, in the last seven games of the 1972 season at Lawrenceville School we scored 20 touchdowns on passing from the basic single wing formation, and we have had many other highly productive years.

To be sure, we have not thrown as many passes as some teams, but we have had a high percentage of completions and a low percentage of interceptions. Obviously we have done much better when we have had good passers at tailback and wingback (and sometimes at fullback as well). Regardless of our passers' ability, we have stressed certain points that have helped us immeasurably.

First of all, we have designed plays on which the passer has only one option. One reason this is feasible is that so many times our passes evolve from tailback or wingback running plays in which two receivers are in the passer's line of sight. On these plays the passer may be trained to look for the deep receiver, and if he's covered, look for the short receiver, or he may look for a certain receiver, and if he's covered, run the ball. This progression can, of course, be reversed: e.g., Run the ball if possible or throw to a short receiver. Whatever options there are, the passer will be trained to use them correctly, and he will have plenty of practice reading the defensive players involved.

Another rule we emphasize for our passers is "Don't throw a short pass long, and don't throw a long pass short." We do more than pay lip service to this rule: We stress it every day in practice, explaining in each case where to throw and, if necessary, where to throw the pass away. When we go counter to this rule, we often get interceptions. This is easily demonstrated on the practice field and when viewing game films.

Developing the Young Passer

Information for training passers is readily available in clinic notes, books, and articles. Leaning on these sources, we have used such standard drills as throwing from one knee as a warm-up, the circle drill, and the "across the field drill," which we mentioned when discussing tailback techniques in Chapter 3. The last drill—in which two boys run back and forth across the field 10 yards apart, throwing and catching the football—is particularly helpful to tailbacks and wingbacks because they throw so many running passes. These drills help develop flexibility in the upper body. I will mention them again later in the chapter.

There are some other fundamental drills that are equally helpful to young passers. Topnotch college and pro passers grip the football in many different ways, but all of them seem to have strong fingers and a deft sense of touch. An extremely helpful activity, therefore, is what we call the "drop drill." In this drill the boy should pick up a ball from the ground, using only his fingertips. *The palm does not touch the football.* He next drops the ball a couple of inches but quickly grasps it with his fingers before it touches the ground. This drill helps strengthen the fingers and helps develop the boy's sense of touch, which is so important to a passer.

On dropback passes, the single wing passer must learn to take the center pass, mold the ball in his hands (as he fixes his passing grip), and raise the ball high in both hands in a passing stance. Next he must do this and learn to step with his front foot in the direction of his throw. The passer must also learn to take a lead pass from center and mold the ball ready to throw on the run.

When you progress to practicing pass patterns, you must be realistic about not moving too quickly with young passers and receivers. Obviously you cannot introduce too many pass patterns right away but instead must strive to perfect a small number. You can add more patterns as the season progresses. At any one time you cannot work with more than two or three tailbacks and more than two or three sets of receivers. And you cannot try to work intensively on both pass offense and pass defense at the same time if you want to get anywhere with your passing game.

Dropback Passes
Protection

The first priority in designing any passing attack is protection for the passer. With minimum splits in the line and the tailback already some 5 yards deep, the single wing has built-in advantages over any T passing attack. For any dropback pass, we have only one protection, whether right formation or left formation.

The passer aligns in close position (left foot on the ball in right formation, right foot on the ball in left formation) at 5 yards' depth. He is just about in the middle of his protection now. He moves back a step or two behind No. 5 as he catches the ball, gets on balance, and steps up to deliver the ball. The linemen, from No. 3 to No. 7, stay square and allow no defensive lineman to penetrate inside of them.

Each lineman shoots his hands aggressively into the defensive lineman rushing him, giving ground grudgingly as he uses repeated blows. If the defensive man opposite him is stunting, our lineman must shuffle back slightly in a crouched position and take on the first man who ends up coming toward him. If no rusher attacks a man, he should stay low and retreat along with the adjacent offensive linemen so there is no gap in our protecting wall. With our minimum splits, it is hard to blitz a linebacker between linemen if players use their hands aggressively.

The fullback steps forward and then over to the weakside to block the first defender past the No. 3 lineman. He must not step over and then up because a defender could slice inside of him. The blocking back steps over to take the first rusher past the No. 7 lineman. If the fullback is the passer, the tailback (from far position) takes the fullback's job. This is the protection we use on all dropback passes.

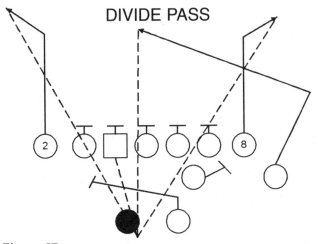

Figure 67

Divide Pass

Figure 67 shows one of our basic patterns we call "Divide Pass." On this play both ends run downfield for about 10 yards, make a head-fake to the inside, and cut sharply to the outside as shown in the diagram. The wingback runs to the outside and cuts into the middle as shown. We designate the receiver by calling the play Divide 2, Divide 8, or Divide Wing. If the end gets a step on the halfback, the passer throws the ball to the outside and deep. He has been trained not to throw a long pass short. Against a two-deep defense, the wingback

should be open in the middle, and this is the way we often attack a two-deep.

Delay Wing Pass

We can also throw to the wingback underneath and between the backers, in which case we call it "Delay Wing." On this pass the wing starts out flatter and then cuts sharply to the shallow middle.

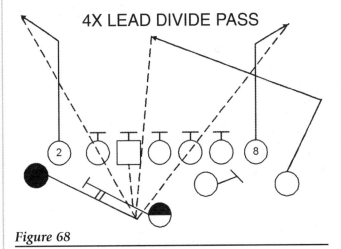

Figure 68

4 X Lead Divide Pass

Another effective variation of this pass is 4X Lead Divide. (See Figure 68.) In this case the tailback is set as a close flanker to the weakside (4X) and runs back on the snap to take the ball from the fullback. The full takes a lead center and runs to the weakside to hand off behind him before setting up to block. As always on dropback protection, the full blocks the first man past No. 3. The fullback aligns behind No. 5 originally, and after taking the handoff, the tail ends up in his usual position for dropback passing behind the No. 5 lineman.

Although we have thrown to both the No. 8 end and the wingback with success on occasion, this variation has been most effective for us when thrown to the No. 2 end (Lead Divide 2). Defensive halfbacks should key pass receivers who release downfield, but high school halfbacks have often been distracted by the tailback running away from them. This variation has given us some long gains.

PRO PASS

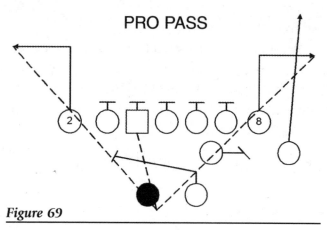

Figure 69

Pro Pass

Another of our favorite patterns is what we call "Pro Pass." As shown in Figure 69, both ends run fast downfield 8 to 10 yards (or whatever is needed for a first down), get under control, and cut to the outside. The wing runs downfield through the defensive halfback. We designate the pass as Pro 2 or Pro 8.

We never throw this pass from one hash mark to the wide side of the field, but instead set the formation, right or left to throw into the narrow side. At the widest, we start from the middle of the field. The passer must throw the ball hard to the receiver's outside so the pass is caught for a first down or thrown out of bounds. If the receiver is covered, we deliberately overthrow out of bounds. From dropback we *never* throw flat to the wide field.

Because teams typically defend us with three deep and a strong safety to the strongside, we most often throw to the No. 2 end (Pro 2) into the narrow side and away from the defensive strength. If the defense has no strong safety or places him always to the wide side, we might set the formation into the narrow side and throw Pro 8. On this play proper passing mechanics are especially important. For example, a right-handed passer must be on balance and step with his left foot in the direction he is throwing. For a right-hander, it is

more difficult to throw to his left than to his right because he may not plant his left foot correctly. We have worked hard to perfect this play, and for many years it has given us crucial first downs, often when we were behind in games and marching downfield to catch up.

QUICK PASSES

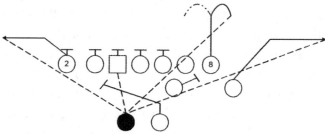

Figure 70

Quick Passes

Similar to the Pro pass is a Quick pattern in which both the No. 2 end and the wingback run into the flat at a depth of only 2 or 3 yards. Figure 70 shows this play, which we call "Quick 2 Flat" or "Quick Wing Flat." To throw a Quick pass, the passer must not fade back at all or pump fake but catch the ball, grip it, and throw. In 1981 at Lawrenceville School we capped a magnificent rally with a two-point extra point on Quick Wing Flat that almost failed because the tailback took too long before throwing. He had to throw high because a defensive man was coming up to cover, but fortunately our wingback, an excellent receiver, was able to make an outstanding leaping catch.

On this play we also have a Quick 8 Hook, on which the 8 end steps forward to turn and catch a short hook pass at about 5 yards' depth. This is a good pass to use against a typical Oklahoma Defense adjusted. I do not like to throw deeper hook passes without a play-action fake because of the danger of a backer suddenly looming up to intercept the ball.

Flat and Up Pass

Closely allied to the Pro and Quick Flat passes are 2 Flat and Up and Wing Flat and

FLAT AND UP PASS

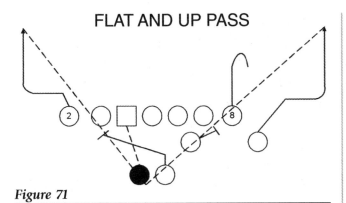

Figure 71

Up. On these passes the receiver runs toward the sideline at a depth of about 4 yards, throws out his hands as if to catch the ball (as the tailback pump fakes), then cuts upfield. Again, we do not want to throw this pass from farther than the middle of the field. It works very well from the hash mark into the narrow side. (See Figure 71.)

QUICK 8 CROSS PASS

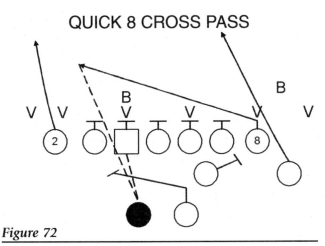

Figure 72

Quick 8 Cross Pass

Another pass that is effective against certain defenses is Quick 8 Cross. This works very well against defenses in which the weakside backer is overcommitted to stop the run, playing up close to the line of scrimmage, in a position shown in Figure 72. Here we have a true undershifted 6, with the weakside backer head-on our center. In an important Lawrenceville game in 1958 we expected this defensive alignment from our opponents, so we prepared Quick 8 Cross as part of our game plan. When the anticipated defense material-

ized, we used this pass to the No. 8 end to great advantage. We completed it twice from right formation for gains of 35 yards and 23 yards and once from left formation for 38 yards.

When you guess correctly and your plans work out, you're a genius. Would that you could do this all the time. My point in discussing this seldom-used pattern is to suggest a way in which you can prepare special plays for given situations you have reason to anticipate. Bear in mind that introducing a special pass like this is not difficult. You have already taught the tailback how to throw a Quick Pass and you are using standard pass protection. But you must practice it a good bit in preparation that week against the anticipated defense.

POST 2 PASS

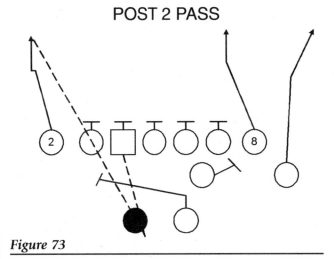

Figure 73

Post 2 Pass

What we call "Post 2 Pass" is another good pattern from the basic formation. We throw many passes of various kinds on which the receiver breaks to the outside. This is especially true of the No. 2 end. Therefore, it's important to have an effective post pattern for that end. Figure 73 shows this play. Again there is regular dropback protection. The No. 2 end, who may flex out a bit, breaks downfield bearing to the outside, head-fakes to the outside, then cuts straight upfield. The No. 8 end occupies the safety and the wing occupies the strongside halfback. The No. 2 end splits the zone between the weakside halfback and the safety to catch the pass.

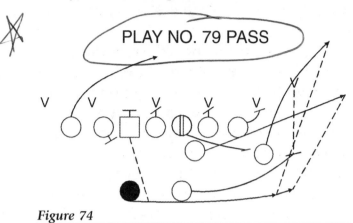

PLAY NO. 79 PASS

Figure 74

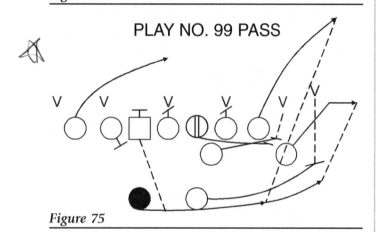

PLAY NO. 99 PASS

Figure 75

Running Pass Plays

The running pass by the tailback is one of the most potent weapons in the single wing arsenal. We have executed the running pass in two similar ways. The last digit of each play is 9, indicating that each can end up wide to the strongside as a run. Blocking assignments on both passes are the same for all interior linemen and for the fullback, who blocks the end man on the line. The plays are similar in design and operate on similar principles. The difference comes in who the two strongside receivers are.

On Play No. 79 Pass (Figure 74), the pattern we have used most, the wingback is a deep receiver running a banana course, and the blocking back is a shallow underneath receiver

running in the flat at about 3 yards' depth. On Play No. 99 Pass (Figure 75), the No. 8 end runs a deep banana route, and the wingback runs a sprintout course at about 3 yards' depth with the blocking back blocking the second man in.

There are good reasons for having two such similar plays. Sometimes we have a real difference in the receiving ability of players. For example, the blocking back may be a poor receiver and we may want to use the wingback in the flat pattern. Also when we line up the wingback on the weakside, we still have a deep outside threat from the No. 8 end with Play No. 99 Pass. Finally, we have found it convenient to designate variations of the running pass by 99 as I'll show in the next part of this chapter.

Play No. 79 Pass

Now I'll discuss Play No. 79 Pass in more detail. From near position (behind the center) the tailback takes a 4 (lead) center and runs under control to the strongside while setting the ball in his hands to pass. We want him to look for his receivers early. Ideally he should be ready to throw by the time he is behind the wingback's original area. The wing must run his banana course *from the start*. He must not run downfield and then veer to the outside or the safety can rotate over and pick him up while the halfback moves up to cover underneath. If the wing is open, the tail throws him a high, soft pass over his outside shoulder. The blocking back runs at the defensive end and then slides into the flat.

Both the wing and the blocking back are effective receivers on this play, and both are in the tailback's line of vision. The tail can look to throw to the wing first and, if he's covered, throw to the blocking back. Or on what we call a "79 Run It," he can expect to run the ball unless he's rushed, in which case he throws to the blocking back. We practice these possibilities and thus can easily adapt to the way the defense is playing. As I said earlier, I never want the passer to have more than one option.

Here are the other assignments for Play No. 79 Pass. The No. 8 end blocks any man in his area, usually the second man in. No. 7 blocks anyone from his outside seam to head-on No. 6. The No. 6 lineman pulls with some depth and blocks where needed. However, he must not pull against packed defenses but instead must block the man on him. The reason: No. 7 cannot block men on both himself and No. 6. The No. 5 lineman blocks anyone from his outside seam to head up. The center blocks any man on him. The No. 3 lineman blocks anyone on him or (if no man on him) the first lineman to the weakside. The No. 2 end runs through the short middle zone as a receiver.

For many years we used a three-man pattern on Play No. 79 Pass with the No. 8 end going straight downfield about 8 yards and then cutting sharply to the outside. We sometimes had success in hitting this receiver. In one Lawrenceville School game in 1971, the No. 8 end caught four passes for good yardage on this play, but we don't usually have that kind of player at tight end. In recent years we have had the No. 8 end block any man in his area. This gives us maximum protection and allows the tailback to focus in a progression on the wingback deep and the blocking back in the shallow flat. With practice, a schoolboy passer can handle this simplified task.

Variations of the Running Pass
Play No. 99-8 Cross Pass

From the basic single wing formation we have used a number of variations of the running pass, each of which is designated by 99 and uses 99 blocking. I will discuss four of these variations here. Over the years the most effective of these passes has been Play No. 99-

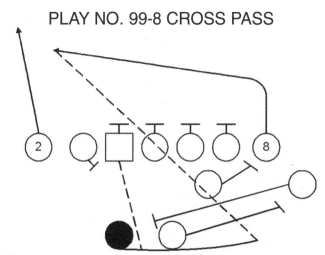

PLAY NO. 99-8 CROSS PASS

Figure 76

8 Cross. Figure 76 shows this play. From near position the tailback takes a 4 (lead) center and runs under control to the strongside as he looks to the outside. We say he "runs with baby steps," giving the illusion of running fast, until he pulls up to throw approximately behind the No. 8 end's original area. At that point he pivots and balances up to throw a lead pass to the No. 8 end crossing over at a depth of 5 or 6 yards.

All the linemen have Play No. 99 assignments except that the No. 6 does not pull, but stays in to block as he does on all 99 variations. The blocking back must not use dropback pass protection blocking but must move out aggressively to block any defender in the No. 8 end's original area. He is an important false key to move the linebackers and the safety to the strongside. Along with the movement of the tailback (with the ball) and the fullback, the blocking back exerts a considerable draw to the strongside. The wingback runs to the weakside to pull up behind the tailback, and he and the fullback, who stops to block, form a protective pocket for the tail. The No. 2 end runs downfield to clear out the defensive halfback.

For years this pass has been consistently successful. It has given us many big plays, including a number of touchdowns and successful 2-point PAT plays. We have used it effectively from both right and left formation. In our most satisfying victory of the 1993 Lawrenceville School season, we completed this pass five times out of five attempts for a total of 68 yards. From right formation we completed it for 14 yards (and a touchdown), 30 yards, and 15 yards. From left formation we had two completions: 3 yards (for a 2 point PAT) and 6 yards (for a touchdown).

PLAY NO. 99-SWITCH PASS

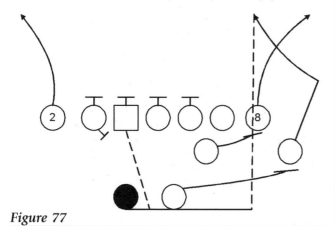

Figure 77

Play No. 99-Switch Pass

Another tried-and-true single wing play we have used successfully is what we call "99-Switch." Figure 77 shows this play. From near position the tailback takes a 4 (lead) center and runs under control to a place behind the No. 8 end's original area to stop and throw a pass to the wingback, who runs out to the strongside before cutting back sharply to the middle of the field. This pass cannot be floated but must be thrown sharply. The No. 8 end runs a banana course, and he and the wing—along with the flow of the tailback, fullback, and blocking back—establish the kind of initial strongside movement we get with the running pass. The No. 3 lineman must block effectively to protect the tail's backside. The No. 2 end runs through the weakside defensive halfback to pull him away from the middle.

With a right-handed passer at tailback, this play should be executed from right formation.

PLAY NO. 99-POST PASS

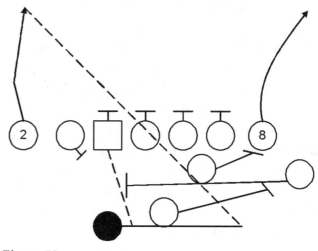

Figure 78

Play No. 99-Post Pass

Figure 78 shows Play No. 99-Post Pass, which (like 99-Switch) is a running pass variation that is designed to take advantage of a safety man who rotates with flow. From near position the tailback takes a 4 (lead) center and runs under control to a place behind the No. 8 end's original area, where he stops to throw to the No. 2 end. That end runs a post pattern, bearing to the outside and giving an outside fake before cutting sharply upfield. The blocking is identical with that on Play No. 99-8 Cross. There is enough flow to get the safety man rotating to the strongside. If the No. 2 end will run a good pattern, he can get a step on the weakside halfback to the inside, where the tail can reach him with a crisply thrown pass at a depth of 20 to 25 yards.

As on 99-8 Cross, the blocking back must run hard to block any man in the No. 8 end's original area. He is an excellent false key to help move the linebackers to the strongside and out of the area where the pass is thrown.

This is a much safer play than Play No. 99-Switch, on which there is always the danger of a linebacker's drifting back unseen and picking off a pass. Therefore, in recent years we have used it instead of Play No. 99-Switch. We have excellent protection for the passer on this play, and it can be used effectively from both left and right formation.

PLAY NO. 99-SCREEN PASS

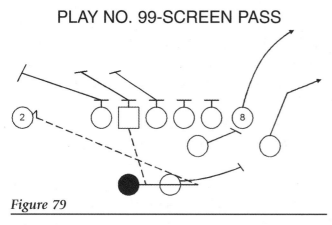

Figure 79

Play No. 99-Screen Pass

One more running pass variation that deserves to be included here is Play No. 99-Screen, a throwback screen from the tailback to the weakside end, who has split out some 10 yards. (See Figure 79.) With a right-handed passer this play should be used from right formation. The tailback accepts a 4 (lead) center and takes three steps (right, left, right) before whirling around to throw to the No. 2 end. That end takes two steps forward before coming back to catch the ball. He should come back to the line of scrimmage to face the tail as he catches the ball. This pass should not be floated but should be thrown crisply. Naturally we do not want to use 99-Screen if there is double coverage on the split No. 2 end.

Here are the line assignments. The No. 3 lineman fakes his normal pass protection block for one count before sprinting out to block the defensive halfback. He will either block the halfback to the outside, if that defender reacts up quickly, or he will lead the receiver downfield as a blocker. The center and No. 5 lineman fake normal pass protection blocks before sprinting out to lead the receiver downfield. The No. 6 and No. 7 lineman have

the same assignments they do on Play No. 99. After some practice this pass is not difficult to execute. It has paid big dividends for us. I wish we had used it more often.

PLAY NO. 40 PASS

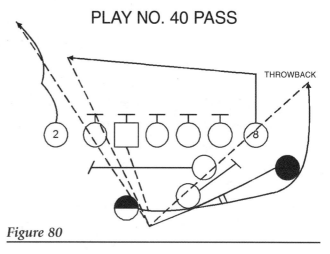

THROWBACK

Figure 80

Reverse Passes

Nothing in our offense has been more important than reverse passes. Over the years they have given us countless big plays and have been the deciding factor in many games. We have two different reverse pass patterns thrown by the wingback from both right and left formation. On Play No. 40 Pass the tailback takes a 4 (lead) center and hands the ball off forward to the wingback. (Figure 80 shows Play No. 40 Pass.) On Play No. 21 Pass the fullback accepts a 2 center and hands behind him to the wingback as he does on 21 Power. I will discuss 21 Pass shortly.

Play No. 40 Pass

Years ago we pulled a lineman on 40 pass as we do on reverse runs. However, for some time now we have used Zero (dropback) protection for the line. This gives us excellent protection, and there is nothing new to teach. From near position the tailback takes the center pass and hands forward to the wingback (with his left hand in right formation) before continuing on his throwback course. The wing stops to throw from a spot 4 or 5 yards behind No. 5. The blocking back crosses over to set up to block the first defensive man past the No. 3 lineman. The full moves out to block the first man past the No. 7 lineman. In order to reach this position without colliding with the wing, the full should align himself about 2 feet closer to the line than usual.

The No. 2 end, the primary receiver, must do his job correctly. He starts downfield with short steps looking at the halfback's feet as if to block him. After about 5 or 6 yards, the No. 2 end bursts into high gear, sprinting to his outside. The wing should loft the ball over that end's outside shoulder as soon as possible with a high, soft pass of some 20 to 25 yards. He must not wait too long to throw, and he must not "throw a long pass short." Overthrowing the receiver will not hurt us, but above all we do not want an interception. The No. 8 end, who runs downfield about 7 yards and then crosses over behind the linebackers, should be in the passer's line of sight and is an outlet receiver. But since we used this pass on normal running downs and not in long yardage, we usually preferred to have the wing let fly and take our chances on a long-gainer.

We know that with practice our wingback is able to throw this sort of pass adequately. It also helps the surprise element if we have a left-handed passer from right formation, but this is not essential. A right-handed passer can take a handoff and stop to throw 40 Pass from right formation as well as left formation. We have often substituted a tailback at wingback to get an extra passer in the game for this play. With a little planning you can teach that sub wingback a couple of other plays to disguise your intentions.

This play has paid big dividends. Here is an indication of its longevity: In the last game of our 1956 Lawrenceville School season we used it to complete a 21-yard touchdown pass, and in the last game of the 1999 season it was good for a 24-yard touchdown pass. There were many touchdowns in between.

Play No. 40 Throwback Pass

From this pass pattern we have also had good success with Play No. 40 Throwback. We like to throw this pass into the narrow side of the field. The wingback takes an inside handoff, sets up in the pocket while looking toward the No. 2 end, then pivots to throw back to the tailback. The key to the success of the play comes after the handoff when the tail slows down in a nonchalant manner as he turns the corner before looking for the pass. He must be a good actor. A defensive halfback has a tendency to ignore the tailback when he slows down after handing off to the wingback. (See Figure 80.)

We have used this variation sparingly, but like the parent play it has been good to us for a long time. It was never more effective than in the 1996 season when on successive Saturdays we had completions of a 31-yard touchdown pass from right formation and a 5-yard scoring pass from left formation. Interestingly enough, our right-handed wingback threw both passes.

PLAY NO. 21 PASS

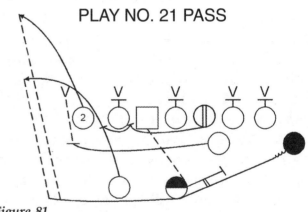

Figure 81

Play No. 21 Pass

Now for a discussion of our other reverse pass, Play No. 21 Pass: Unlike 40 Pass, on which we use dropback protection, this is a running reverse pass that is part of the 20 series. (See Figure 81.)

The fullback takes a 2 center (to his right knee in right formation) and half-spins to hand the ball off to the wingback. As with other 20 series plays, the wing starts a count early in quick motion. If you are not featuring the 20 series, the wing does not have to start a count early. After handing off, the fullback stays in place to block anyone chasing the wingback from behind. From far position the tailback runs inside the defensive end and into the weakside flat at about 5 yards' depth. The blocking back lines up deeper than usual and blocks the defensive end. At times we have lined him up in Q position, directly behind the No. 3 lineman, to get a better blocking angle on that end.

The No. 2 end runs a banana course *from the start*. He must not go straight downfield first and then veer outside or the safety can rotate over to cover him while the halfback goes up to cover the tail. If that end gets free, the wing must throw him a high, soft pass over his outside shoulder. Of course, if he throws to the tailback, he must not float the ball.

Now for the line blocking: We no longer include the No. 8 end in the pattern but use him as a blocker. He blocks anyone on him or close outside. If we face a packed defense, he must block to the inside first. The No. 7 lineman blocks the man on the No. 6 lineman to the man on him, in order of priority. If necessary, he must first fill for No. 6, who makes a shallow pull to the weakside.

As shown in the diagram, after he pulls, the No. 6 looks first to block any defensive man in the seam between the No. 3 lineman and the center and, if there's no one there, he looks to block anyone close outside of the No. 3 lineman. Since the No. 3 is assigned to block the second man in and often steps to the outside, we don't want to let a blitzer through into our backfield. The No. 5 lineman blocks any man on him or, if no man on him, braces up. The center follows the same blocking rules as No. 5. This line protection has worked well.

Whether thrown to the No. 2 end deep or to the tailback in the flat, 21 Pass has given us many successful plays. None was more memorable than the 10-yard touchdown completion to the tailback in the last 15 seconds to win our biggest victory of the 1962 season at Wabash College. This pass was thrown from right formation by a left-handed wingback, which brings up an important point.

There is no doubt that, for an inexperienced wingback passer, it is easier for a left-hander to throw a running reverse pass from right formation and a right-hander to throw this pass from left formation. But with practice we have often had right-handed wingbacks throw successfully while running to their left.

It's a matter of flexibility in the upper body, which we develop in our wingbacks and tailbacks in the "across the field" drill we use regularly at the beginning of practice. This drill has really helped us. In one Lawrenceville School game in 1972 our right-handed wingback, running to his left, completed Play No. 21 Pass four times, twice to the No. 2 end and twice to the tailback. So this technique can be mastered.

PLAY NO. 21 X PASS

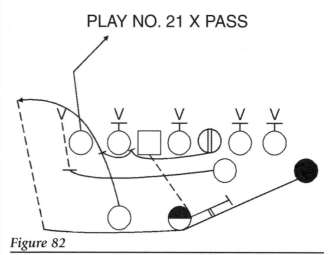

Figure 82

Play No. 21 X Pass

There is one variation of the reverse running pass we have sometimes used with success going for a 2-point extra point or when we are close to the goal line. In that part of the field some teams always use a man-for-man pass defense. We call this variation "21 X pass." (See Figure 82.) This is virtually the same play as before except that, instead of running a banana course, the No. 2 end now runs at the halfback who is covering him and pulls him to the inside. The tailback is now the only receiver the wing looks for. If the tail is covered, the wing runs with the ball. Used at the right time, this pass variation can win you a game.

Play-Action Passes

We move now to a discussion of play-action passes, which have been highly effective when used from the single wing offense. Here are a few we have used with success. It's easy to add other passes, but bear in mind you can practice and perfect only a limited number at any one time.

The 80 Series

We have already talked about the 80 series with respect to running plays, but this series is especially effective for play-action passes. The beauty of this series is that it is easy to install and still gives us a good action fake that holds the linebackers in position so you can throw behind them into the middle zone. As I've said before, I do not like to throw into the middle without a fake of this sort because of the danger of interceptions.

Play No. 80-2 Cross Pass

Figure 83 shows what we call "2 Cross," one of our best 80 series passes. The blocking for the interior linemen and the blocking back is identical with what they do on dropback protection, and the fullback has the same assignment although he gets into position differently. All players are reminded it's this type of protection because it's a Zero pass. From close position, left foot on the ball in right formation, the tailback takes an 8 center

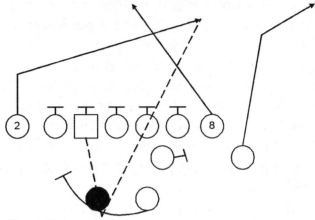

PLAY NO. 80-2 CROSS PASS

Figure 83

to his right knee. He steps up with his right foot to catch the ball, half-spins to fake to the fullback, then steps back into the pocket behind the No. 5 lineman. The full makes a good fake of taking the ball from the tail and then steps up to his regular dropback protection position, where he will block the first man past the No. 3 lineman as usual.

The wing runs through the halfback on his side, and the No. 8 end runs through the safety. The No. 2 end, the designated receiver, runs downfield about 4 or 5 yards and cuts sharply across to the strongside, gaining some depth as he goes. The tail hits him in full stride after he has crossed behind the strongside backer. To widen the receiving area, we have sometimes flanked the wing out 10 yards or more to the strongside (A), from where he still runs through the defensive halfback. In that case we call the play "A 80-2 Cross." (See Chapter 8.)

Play No. B 80-8 Cross Pass

Figure 84 shows a companion play we have used: B 80-8 Cross. Now the wing is flanked to the weakside (B), from where he runs through the halfback on his side, and the No. 2 end runs through the safety. The No. 8 end, the designated receiver, runs downfield 4 or 5 yards and cuts sharply across to the weakside,

PLAY NO. B 80-8 CROSS PASS

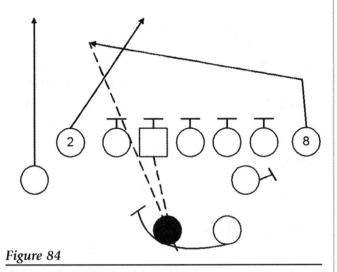

Figure 84

gaining some depth as he goes. The tail hits him in full stride after he has crossed behind the weakside backer. The blocking assignments for all players remain the same as does the tailback-fullback faking. Depending on what we are doing offensively, we have used passes like these from variations A and B to blend in with other plays. (See Chapter 8.)

PLAY NO. 80-DIVIDE WING PASS

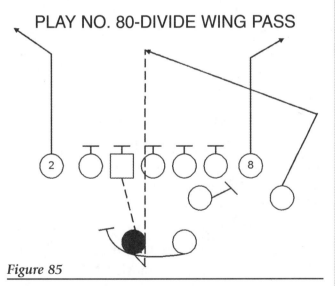

Figure 85

Play No. 80-Divide Wing Pass

One other 80 series pass has been highly effective against a 2-deep defense: 80-Divide Wing. Figure 85 shows this play. Now we run the Divide Wing pattern I discussed earlier with 80 series mechanics. If we face a 2-deep de-

fense, both ends will pull the halfbacks to the outside and the wingback should be open in the middle zone. The tailback-fullback fake momentarily keeps the backers from retreating into pass defense.

The 20 Series

When we utilize 20 series passes, the player in the fullback position will take a 2 center to his right knee, fake with a half spin to the wingback as usual, and step back to pass. The boy in the tailback spot will block the first man past the No. 3 lineman in typical dropback protection. We may have the regular fullback do the passing, *if* he is a passer, or more often we have the tailback and the fullback switch positions so the tail can do the passing. The linemen and the blocking back have their normal dropback protection assignments since, again, this is a Zero pass.

PLAY NO. 20-COUNTER PASS

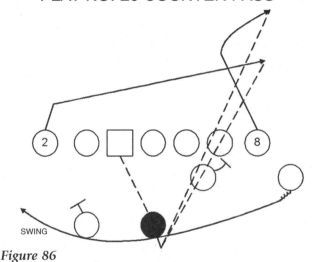

Figure 86

Play No. 20-Counter Pass

Figure 86 shows Play No. 20-Counter Pass, a play that illustrates how the 20 series works. This pass is used against teams that rotate the secondary when we send the wing in quick motion. The No. 8 end, the primary receiver, runs to the inside and then cuts sharply to the outside as shown in the diagram. If he's open, the passer throws him a high, soft pass over his outside shoulder. The No. 2 end runs a crossing route underneath, and he is an option for the passer. When we throw to the wing on a swing pattern, it is a designated play called beforehand.

The 30 Series

Like the 20 series, 30 series passes are thrown by the boy in the fullback position, whether he is the regular full or the tail, if the two players switch positions. Since the last digit is again Zero, all players know this signifies dropback protection.

The fullback, who lines up behind the No. 5 lineman, takes a 3 center to his left knee, and as he catches the ball, he takes a short step with his left foot and then a longer step with his right foot. He continues moving, pivoting on the ball of his right foot and turns around and stops momentarily with his back to the line while the tail and the wing run by. Then he steps back to pass. Those two backs fake taking the ball as they do on 34. After his good fake, the wing takes a couple of steps and then balances up to block the first defensive man past the No. 3 lineman.

Play No. 30-Ends Cross Pass

Figure 87 shows Play No. 30-Ends Cross Pass. The wing starts a count early as he al-

ways does on quick motion in the 30 series. The No. 8 end starts crossing over at once, while the No. 2 end goes downfield 4 or 5 yards before crossing over. The tail throws a high, soft pass to the No. 2 end. For best results this pass should be used on a running down. In a 1998 Lawrenceville School game, with our opponents expecting a running play, we completed this pass for a 60-yard touchdown. (This exact pattern may also be used from the 20 series: 20-Ends Cross Pass.)

Special Passes

In this section I will discuss special passes, plays that do not fit into any of the usual categories of passes and are utilized sparingly when needed. I'll list five of these plays we have used successfully. My hope is that coaches will find some helpful ideas here.

PLAY NO. 48 JUMP PASS

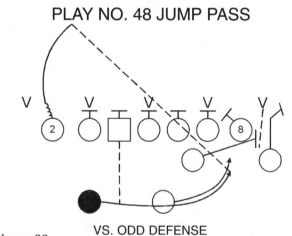

VS. ODD DEFENSE

Figure 88

Play No. 48 Jump Pass

I will begin here with Play No. 48 Jump Pass. Figure 88 shows this play. It is not as difficult to execute as some may think, but it does require considerable practice time. Consequently, there have been many seasons when I just didn't include it in our offense. You can teach only so much.

Except for the element of the jump pass itself, which involves only the tail and the No. 2 end, all assignments are identical with those on Play No. 48, the regular off-tackle play. All

PLAY NO. 30-ENDS CROSS PASS

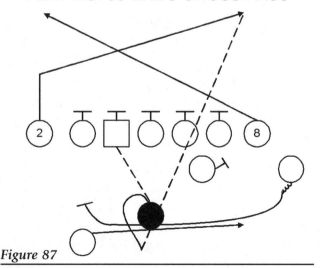

Figure 87

players block aggressively. From far position the tail takes a 4 center and follows the fullback, running an arc downfield as he does on Play No. 48. As with Play No. 99-8 Cross, he runs "with baby steps," giving the impression of moving faster than he is actually running. The tail stays low as he approaches the line and then jumps off his left foot to go up in the air and pass to the No. 2 end, who normally goes downfield to block the safety man on the regular off-tackle play. The end should go half speed at the start so as not to get too far downfield. As on Play No. 48, the blocking back moves aggressively to the strongside to trap the first man past the No. 8 end. This play is a highly effective key breaker, especially for backers, who often key the blocking back.

We have usually used 48 Jump Pass as a deterrent to overaggressive linebackers, giving us short gains without much element of risk. We have also used it as a scoring pass near the goal line, especially on 2-point PAT plays. Ordinarily we do not expect long gains on this play, but in a 1966 Wabash College game we hit the jackpot for a 77-yard touchdown play.

Here was the situation. We had second down and 5 yards to go on our own 23-yard line and our opponents, expecting a run, were in a man-to-man defense in the secondary. The safety and the strong halfback were keying our No. 8 end and wing respectively, so they moved up quickly to help stop what looked like an off-tackle play. Our No. 2 end caught the pass, got a step on the weak halfback, and was off to the races. A play like that is good for the soul.

Delay 8 Pass

A special pass we have depended upon over the years is what we call "Delay 8." (See Figure 89.) Like the Delay Wing I've already discussed (See Page 59), we use this play to pick up a first down. We don't expect to make a long gain with it. This is an easy pass to teach, and

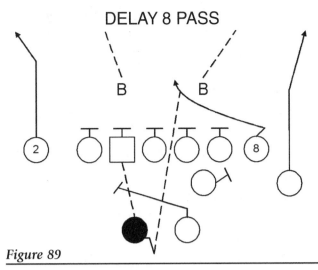

Figure 89

it is highly effective. We use standard dropback protection. Both the wing and the No. 2 end flex out a bit, as they often do in passing situations, and run straight downfield. The tail takes the center, sets up to pass, and looks deep downfield. The No. 8 end hesitates in place, faking a block for two counts, before finding a free space between the backers to catch the pass. Usually that end is tackled quickly, but we expect to have a first down. If used sparingly so the backers don't anticipate this pass, it is highly dependable.

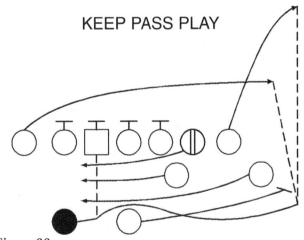

Figure 90

The Keep Pass Play

The next play I will discuss is what we call the "Keep Pass." This is sometimes called the "Bootleg Pass." (See Figure 90.) Like the Keep running play I discussed in Chapter 4, on the strongside this play closely resembles Play No. 43, the inside reverse. The difference comes in the fake handoff between the tailback and the wingback and the tail's subsequent pass to the No. 8 end.

The No. 7 lineman, the blocking back, and the wing execute their 43 assignments although now the wing fakes taking the ball from the tail. (For teams keying the blocking back, this is another key breaker.) The other interior linemen brace up in place to prevent penetration. From far position the tailback accepts a 4 center and extends the ball forward to the wingback with his left hand and then moves it behind his back to his right hand. This fake of showing the ball helps lure the end man on the line to the inside, setting up the fullback's block.

The tail runs under control, but the wing runs hard by him as he makes a realistic fake of taking the ball. You can have the wing start a count early in quick motion, depending on what you are doing with the offense. I prefer the quick motion because it helps set up the pass to the No. 8 end. That end goes downfield for about 5 yards and then veers out to get outside and behind the defensive halfback. The tail should get ready to throw as quickly as possible after his fake to the wing.

This kind of pass should be used on a running down. In the diagram the No. 2 end is an underneath receiver crossing over. When we look at the films, the No. 2 end is often open, but our tailback has never completed a pass to him, and in truth I'd prefer to have him think about hitting the No. 8 end deep. When you do complete this pass to the No. 8 end, it can pay huge dividends. In one of our biggest victories at Wabash College in 1962, we completed this pass for a 57-yard gain.

Solo Pass

We have already discussed Solo, a running play on which the tailback, from far position,

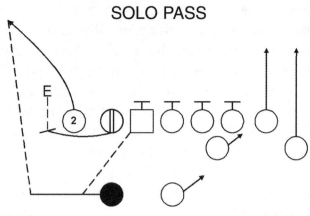

SOLO PASS

Figure 91

takes a direct lead to the weakside and runs outside. Like that running play, Solo Pass depends completely on the element of surprise. (See Figure 91.) You are assuming the weakside defensive end just doesn't expect the tail to run outside with a direct lead. While we have used the running play from both left and right formation, it is much easier for a right-handed tailback to throw this pass from left formation running to his right, and that is the way I have used this play. As I said in my discussion of Solo as a running play, the center will need special practice to make this lead to the weakside.

The place to use this pass play is near the goal line because in that area of the field the weakside defensive halfback tends to come up quickly on any flow to the outside. The No. 2 end runs a quick banana route to get behind that halfback. The tailback runs to the outside getting ready to throw to the No. 2 end as soon as possible. The No. 3 lineman pulls to block the defensive end, who often plays tight near the goal line. It doesn't make too much difference what our other players do on this seldom-used play though we have always had the blocking back and fullback sprint to the strongside. The element of surprise is the important thing. This highly improbable play gave us a touchdown in a 1998 Lawrenceville School game.

PLAY NO. 3X-63 SHOVEL PASS

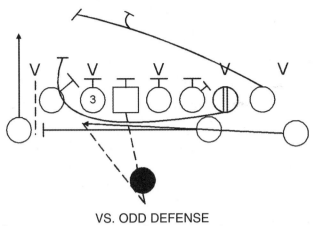

VS. ODD DEFENSE

Figure 92

Play No. 3X-63 Shovel Pass

Like other styles of offense, the single wing has always used shovel passes. Figure 92 shows 3X-63 Shovel Pass, a good performer for us over the years. Like a Statue of Liberty play, which I will discuss shortly, a shovel pass does two things for your offense: First, it gives you a dependable play that can catch the defense off balance. Second, it's the kind of offbeat play kids enjoy practicing. The element of fun can be important in a long practice.

Because we like to get "two for the price of one," we are glad to use standard 3-hole blocking on this play. As the diagram shows, all linemen and the blocking back have assignments that are identical with other 3-hole plays. In this diagram I placed the fullback as a close weakside flanker, so we now call the play "3X-63 Shovel." From that position the fullback can widen the hole, an aid to the blocking back's trap. The full, when flanked, can also loosen up the weakside halfback as he runs downfield.

From close position the tail accepts a 6 (straight-back) center, raises the ball in both hands, and throws a soft pass to the wing, who has run under control behind the line. The tail must make sure the pass is not too hard for the wing to handle. Therefore, he flicks a pass with his wrist without following through, hit-

ting his receiver as he is behind the double team block. We consider this to be a safe pass as we have never suffered an interception using it.

Fake Passes

In the category of fake passes I am including five plays we have found useful. Perhaps coaches can pick up an idea or two here that will be helpful.

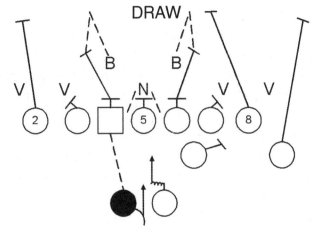

VS. ODD DEFENSE

Figure 93

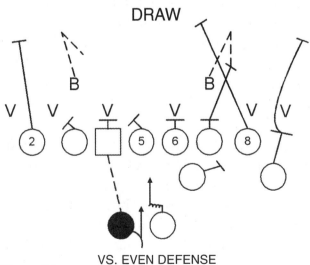

VS. EVEN DEFENSE

Figure 94

The Draw Play

Like other styles of offense, the single wing can effectively utilize the draw play. A draw play is usually used in long yardage against aggressive pass rushers. It is a delayed running

73

play after an initial fake of a pass. Figures 93 and 94 show our draw play against different defenses. From close position the tailback takes a 6 (straight-back) center, fades back a couple of steps looking downfield with the ball raised, then bursts through a hole in the line that is made by steering rushing defensive linemen to desired positions.

Both ends and the wing run downfield as though going for a pass and then block defensive secondary men. As usual, the blocking back blocks the first man past the No. 7 lineman. The fullback steps in front of the tailback and checks for a rusher coming from the weakside. If there is a rusher coming, he steps out to block him. If there is no weakside threat, he leads the tail through the line. These backfield and end assignments remain constant regardless of the defense opposing us.

This play works best against an odd defense. In that case the No. 5 lineman uses his hands to steer the rushing nose man to one side or the other. If the nose does not rush, he must block him to one side or the other. The No. 3 and No. 7 linemen use their hands to steer the men on them to the outside. If these defensive linemen do not rush, we must block them to the outside. The uncovered linemen, No. 6 and the center, fake a pass protection block for one full count and then run to block the backers.

Against an even defense the No. 6 lineman has the key block. He tries to steer the rushing defensive lineman playing on him to the strongside, but No. 6 will have to block him whichever way he wants to go. The No. 5 lineman blocks the defensive man playing on the center to the weakside with the center's help. The No. 7 lineman, who is uncovered, fakes a pass protection block for a full count and then runs out to block the strongside backer. All other assignments are as before on this play, which gives us a potent inside running threat in long yardage situations.

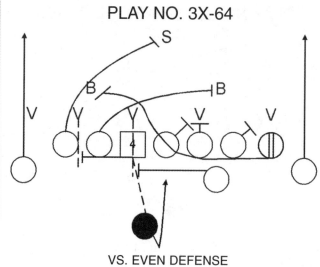

PLAY NO. 3X-64

VS. EVEN DEFENSE

Figure 95

Play No. 3X-64

If you do not have time to teach the draw, an easier way to get an inside fake-pass play is Play No. 3X-64. (See Figure 95.) The fullback, flanked to the weakside (3X), and the wingback run downfield as potential pass receivers and then block the defensive halfback on their side. They should both flex out a bit beforehand as they often would on pass plays. You can place the fullback and the wingback at different positions if you like. Now comes the easy part: All linemen and the blocking back have the same assignments as on any 4-hole play. The tailback accepts a 6 (straight-back) center, quickly raises the ball in both hands as if to pass, and runs into the 4 hole. This play, which is easy to teach, gives you a strong inside running threat in a passing situation.

Play No. 3X-63

Another easy fake-pass-run play to teach is 3X-63. (See Figure 96.) All linemen and the blocking back have their regular 3-hole assignments. The fullback, again flanked to the weakside (3X), and the wingback run downfield as possible receivers and block the defensive halfback on their side. From close position the tailback takes a 6 (straight-back)

PLAY NO. 3X-63

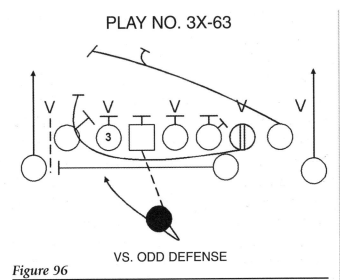

VS. ODD DEFENSE

Figure 96

center, raises the ball in both hands as if passing, and runs into the 3 hole behind the pulling No. 7. I have used this play from time to time since 1956. It can be executed easily from both left and right formations.

FULLBACK SCREEN

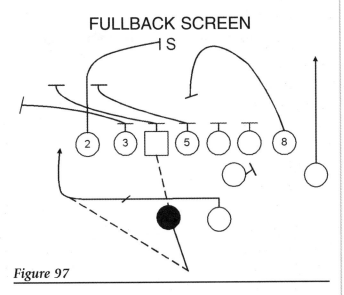

Figure 97

The Fullback Screen

Like other offensive systems, the single wing employs all sorts of screen passes. Typically they are used against aggressive pass rushers in long yardage situations. Over the years our most effective screen has been one to the fullback in the weakside area. (See Figure 97.) For some reason, this play has worked better from left formation than from right formation. It is easy to give the assignments for all players, but it takes plenty of practice to perfect a screen. It goes without saying that the fullback should be a good open-field runner for this screen to be effective.

The tailback takes a 6 (straight-back) center and fades back deeper than usual, looking downfield as if to pass. He then throws to the fullback in the weakside area. The full must cross over to block as usual on a dropback pass and make glancing contact with the rushing defensive end before sliding off and going out to stop and catch the pass. A boy may want to avoid contact with the end, but if he does that, he'll give away the play.

The wing runs off the halfback on his side. The No. 8 end runs downfield and then circles back to block behind the original line of scrimmage. The No. 2 end runs downfield and then turns in to block the safety. The No. 6 and No. 7 linemen and the blocking back have their regular dropback protection assignments. The weakside linemen pass-protect for a full count and then run downfield as blockers in front of the fullback as shown in the diagram.

STATUE

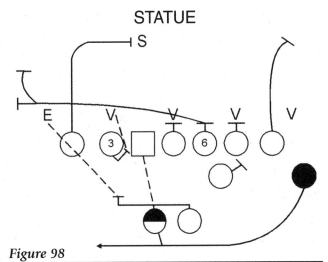

Figure 98

The Statue

The last of the plays I will offer in the category of fake passes is the Statue of Liberty. In addition to being fun to practice, the Statue has been a consistent play for us for many years. (See Figure 98.) Although we have used it from left formation, it is obviously easier for a right-handed tailback from right formation. As we'll see in the next chapter, these assignments are identical with what we use on the handback with a fake quick kick, giving us two excellent plays "for the price of one."

We have definite assignments on the Statue. The No. 2 end runs downfield and then blocks in on the safety. The No. 8 end runs downfield and then blocks the strongside defensive halfback. The center and the No. 5 and No. 7 linemen pass-protect. The No. 6 lineman braces up quickly and then sprints across shallow to block for the wingback. The blocking back steps over to block the first rusher past No. 7 as usual. The full and the No. 3 lineman entice rushers to the inside as shown in the diagram. They are the key blockers. The wing must get early depth so he can level off before taking the ball from the tail, who has raised the ball with both hands in passing position before holding it out with his right hand. The wing says "now" just before he wants the tail

to lower his right hand to offer him the ball. The tail keeps looking downfield as he holds out the ball. There is no reason to look at the wing.

This maneuver is much easier than some people imagine. It takes a little practice, but kids really enjoy the play. We have been using it in this form since 1958, and we have never had a fumbled handoff. I recommend it highly to any single wing coach who wants to jazz up his offense.

Conclusion

In this chapter I have discussed various categories of the passing game. Like other single wing coaches, I like to run the ball. But we have also had considerable success with the passing game. It has not been possible to cover every pass we've ever used, but the large number of passes I've discussed suggests how extensive this phase of our offense has become. I hope some of the ideas presented here will be helpful.

Chapter 7

The QUICK-KICKING GAME

The quick kick is one of the great plays in football. In this chapter I'll discuss all aspects of the quick-kicking game: why you quick-kick, when to quick-kick, the potential psychological benefit of quick kicks and fake quick kick plays, protection for the quick kick, and teaching the kicker.

While teams using other formations have occasionally used the quick kick, they have usually given it up after a short period of time. The single wing is the ideal formation from which to execute this maneuver. If you are using the single wing offense, you should strongly consider utilizing the quick kick.

Field Position

Everyone connected with football uses the term field position. This includes coaches, players, and fans. Anyone who has watched a game on television has heard announcers or analysts talk about field position. If a team has the ball inside their own 10-yard line, we say they have poor field position. If they have the ball on the opposing 30-yard line, we agree they have good field position. Everyone understands those terms. They agree it's a bad thing to have poor field position and a beneficial thing to have good field position. We agree on those terms because we know that the closer we are to the other team's goal line, the easier it will be to score points.

That much is obvious. Yet when my teams have used the quick kick to control field position, people have often referred to it as a gamble, a sign of weakness, or a desperate measure. Every year since becoming a head coach in 1956, I have used the quick kick. And we've used it a lot. Over that span I'm sure we've quick-kicked at least once in every one of our close games. And, depending on circumstances, we've sometimes quick-kicked as often as four times a game. From the single wing formation I knew we could quick-kick effectively and safely. We usually quick-kicked on third down, but sometimes the situation called for it on other downs.

If we depended on the quick kick that much, we had to work hard to perfect it. We always put in the quick kick on the first day of early practice, and later on we practiced quick kicks and fake quick kicks *live* for a short period every Tuesday, Wednesday, and Thursday. Sometimes I would call for a quick kick when we were backed up and wanted to get the ball out of the danger area. For example, in our biggest Lawrenceville School game in 1956, one of our quick kicks traveled from our 5-yard line to the opposing team's 38-yard line. After the kick stopped rolling, the whole complexion of the game changed. Such a scenario was devastating to the morale of an opposing high school team: One minute they felt they had you in trouble, and the next minute they realized they had to start all over again. Another time, in a 1962 Wabash College game, our tailback quick-kicked from our 26-yard line and when the ball stopped rolling, our opponents had the ball on their own 2-yard line. Talk about controlling field position and controlling morale!

Quick Kicks Can Be Important in Games

In a closely fought Lawrenceville game in 1994, our fullback quick-kicked twice: for 59 yards to the opposing team's 9-yard line and for 54 yards to their 7-yard line. These were two of the key plays in a hard-fought victory. That boy was not a very proficient kicker from punt formation, but when quick-kicking he had the knack of getting the ball over the safety's head and having it roll a considerable distance. Similarly in a 1998 Lawrenceville game a quick kick pinned our opponents on their 1-yard line, and we were able to force a safety on the next play.

With a minute and a half to play in a Lawrenceville game in 1978, we led by a touchdown and had fourth down and inches to go on our 40-yard line. Our opponents, expecting a punt, had their safety man deep. When we came out in regular formation, the safety thought we were going for it and raced toward the line of scrimmage. But we quick-kicked for 51 yards, and when the ball rolled dead on

the opposing 9-yard line, the game was essentially over.

Sometimes there would be a bonus involved when the other team's safety man raced back hurriedly to pick up a rolling ball and fumbled, giving us possession. This has happened a number of times. In the biggest game of our 1965 Wabash season, we quick-kicked from our 1-yard line and the opposing safety inadvertently kicked the ball as he hurriedly tried to pick it up while worrying about our players bearing down on him. The result: We recovered a fumble on our 39-yard line. What a confidence booster! Similarly, in a 1994 Lawrenceville game, a quick kick from our 21-yard line was bobbled by a defensive back picking up the ball, and we recovered on the opposing 14-yard line.

QUICK KICK FORMATION

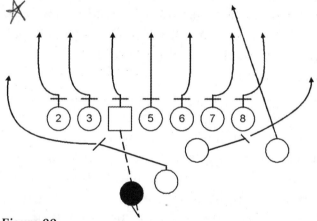

Figure 99

Team Assignments on Our Quick Kick

The individual assignments on the quick kick give us solid protection and excellent coverage. (See Figure 99.) From the No. 3 lineman to the No. 8 end, we take 6-inch splits. Each player anchors his outside foot and steps to the inside, staying low and square and using his hands on rushers. After a solid bump, each player fans out to cover. From the time the center snaps the ball, we should get the kick off in

1.7 seconds. The No. 2 end, split about 2 feet from the No. 3 lineman, blocks any man on him or the first man to his outside before releasing to contain. He too should use his hands on rushers. Wherever the kick goes, the ends have contain responsibility, so they must not run directly to the ball.

Either the tailback or the fullback may be the kicker. In the above diagram the tailback is the kicker. He aligns in close position (left foot on the ball) and takes three steps back before stepping up to kick. The kicker starts backward two counts before the ball is snapped. The fullback steps up and over to block the first man past No. 3 before joining the coverage. As on dropback pass protection, the full must not step over and then up because a rusher could slice inside of him.

QUICK KICK BY FULLBACK

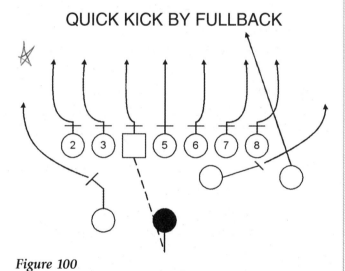

Figure 100

If the fullback is the kicker, he aligns behind the No. 5 lineman and takes three steps back before stepping up to kick. (See Figure 100.) In that case the tail will be in far position (behind No. 3) before stepping up and over to block the first man coming past No. 3. The blocking back must block the first man coming outside the No. 8 end before joining the coverage. We refer to the blocking back and fullback as auxiliary ends. They are contain men behind the No. 8 and No. 2 ends.

The center snaps to the kicker before blocking any rusher and joining his teammates in coverage. His job on quick kicks is obviously much easier than that of the usual long snapper on punts, who must get the ball back 12 or 15 yards with accuracy. This is an easy snap for our center. Our kicker, whether the tail or the full, usually lines up a bit deeper than usual at about 5½ yards depth, but this is not a giveaway because the other player will be lined up even with him.

As shown in the diagram, the wingback is our chase man. He has no blocking or contain responsibilities but races as fast as possible to the ball. We have often aligned the wing split out to the strongside (at A) or to the weakside (at B). But wherever the wing lines up, his job is to track down the ball or the safety with the ball.

We quick-kick from right formation only. It would not be difficult to put in the quick kick from left formation, but it would require valuable practice time. Since we've had excellent results as is, I have never thought it necessary to quick-kick from both left and right formation.

Teaching the Quick Kick Is Not Difficult

From the single wing, it is not difficult to quick-kick. Most boys find it much easier to quick-kick than to punt. On a punt the kicker is usually much deeper. He must catch the long pass from center, which (even with college and pro long snappers) is often not very accurate, and punt the ball high to a safety man. He never knows whether the defense will send an organized punt block at him. On a single wing quick kick, however, the kicker has little fear of a bad center pass or organized pressure from the defense. Assuming that the ball will roll after it lands, all the quick-kicker has to do is get the ball over the head of the safety man, who can only start sprinting back to field the kick on the first backward steps of the kicker.

Both at Wabash College and Lawrenceville School I have been able to teach boys to quick-kick effectively, even those without punting experience. In 1961, our first season at Wabash, the tailback, who had never punted in a game before, learned to quick-kick so well that on 16 kicks he averaged 44 yards per kick from the line of scrimmage. During the same 1961 season the best average for major college punters, who were required to have 24 punts to be counted, was only 42.1 yards. Incidentally, that Wabash tailback never punted for us from regular punt formation all that season. He was the third best punter on a small-college squad.

In my six seasons at Wabash, we never averaged under 40 yards a quick kick. As I indicated earlier in this chapter, we were also successful quick-kicking at Lawrenceville School in 31 seasons. Some of our quick-kickers there were equal to those at Wabash. A coach should not hesitate to use the quick kick at the high school level. Younger players can learn this skill.

Coaching Points in Teaching the Kicker

In this section I will discuss the coaching points I have used since 1956 in teaching the quick kick. Assuming we will quick-kick on the count of three, we want the kicker to take three short steps backward, starting on the count of one. Ideally, in the runback, we'd like our kicker to take his first step backward with his left foot, his second step with his right foot, and his third with his left foot. As the kicker's left foot hits the ground with his last step, we'd like the football to reach him with a low, accurate center pass. From here we'd like him to execute the classic step-and-a-half kick: a short step with the leading right foot, a normal step with the left foot, and the kick with the right

foot. Ideally we'd like our kicker to make contact with the ball from the spot where he originally lined up.

What I've covered above is the ideal situation. You should not over-coach the kicker. Some of our best quick-kickers have used different methods of stepping back in the runback. What's important is that the kicker ends up with sufficient depth and he gets the kick away quickly enough: We never want to get the kick blocked. The other important thing is to *get the right kind of low quick kick that will roll*.

To get that kind of kick, the kicker should *hold the ball low and well out in front of him*. He should lay the ball on his instep, holding the toes of his kicking foot down at the instant of impact. It can be a spiral or an end-over-end kick. If it is a spiral, you definitely don't want the high kind on which the front point noses over. Instead you want the kind of spiral that tails off so the rear point of the ball hits the ground first, giving it a forward impetus that makes it roll. An experienced kicker can often learn to kick the ball to the right or to the left of the retreating safety man, which is an ideal situation. But I would make sure the kicker concentrates on meeting the ball correctly first.

Once you have taught the kicker how to hold the ball and how to place it on his instep, the best drill I know to teach him how to quick-kick (or to punt) is to make him kick to another player in a controlled manner, starting out at 15 or 20 yards and gradually increasing the distance. At such short distances he can concentrate on meeting the ball properly, and he will find that the ball seems to fly off his instep so he often kicks it over the head of the player working with him—invariably with an added roll. This is a confidence-building drill that will convince him he can learn to quick-kick. In these preliminary stages you can also have the kicker learn his backward steps in the runback. Finally, you can have him practice the whole procedure, always making sure he kicks in a controlled manner. With these coaching methods, most of the boys I've worked with have learned to quick-kick effectively. It's not that difficult.

Fake Quick Kick Plays

When a team has been effective with quick kicks, the next logical step is to have a number of fake quick kick plays that can be used occasionally as surprise maneuvers. Fake quick kick plays, of course, are plays in which the tailback takes the same backward steps before the snap as on the quick kick, but then another type of play develops. These plays tend to be successful because with the threat of a quick kick the opposing team often leaves itself vulnerable by having linemen rush recklessly and the secondary retreat quickly.

The variety of fake quick kick plays seems endless because, except for the tailback's fake backward steps, these are many of the same plays we've been using in our regular offense. In this section I will diagram a number of running and passing plays we have used successfully as fake quick kick plays. Once given the idea, a coach can easily add any plays that will take advantage of the strengths of his own offensive personnel and the weaknesses of his opponent's defense.

FAKE QUICK KICK SEAM BUCK (PLAY NO. 16)

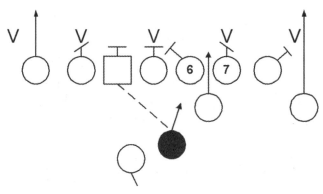

Figure 101

Fake Quick Kick Fullback Bucks

Simple fullback bucks after a backward fake by the tailback can be highly successful. When we run regular seam bucks, the tailback is not directly involved in the play: he merely fakes behind the quick-hitting thrusts by the fullback. Except for the three backward steps by the tailback faking the quick kick, we recognize Play No. 16 in Figure 101. The other seam bucks are equally adaptable. We can also use the fullback wedge as a fake quick kick play. In our biggest game of the 1959 Lawrenceville season, with third down and short yardage, we picked up a vital first down on a fake quick-kick wedge play that allowed us to hang on and preserve a victory.

FAKE QUICK KICK END RUN (PLAY NO. 49)

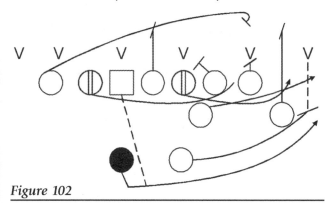

Figure 102

Fake Quick Kick End Run

In our final game of the 1965 Wabash season, we used a different kind of running play that gave us a crucial first down. Our tailback faked a quick kick, then ran around end on Play No. 49. (See Figure 102.) That tailback was a fast, elusive runner, the kind of player who could execute such a play well. A coach should use plays that take advantage of the strengths of his players.

Fake Quick Kick Passes

We like to throw passes after the fake of a quick kick. Fakes of this type force at least part

FAKE QUICK KICK DIVIDE WING PASS

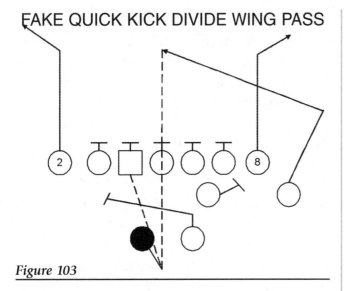

Figure 103

of the secondary to retreat quickly to field the anticipated quick kick, thus weakening the pass defense. The tailback fades backward several steps as if quick-kicking before the snap from center reaches him. Then he straightens up to hit his receiver. Figure 103 shows Divide Wing, a standard single wing pass I've already discussed that is an excellent antidote to a retreating safety man. We've had success with this pass after the fake of a quick kick.

FAKE QUICK KICK 8 CROSS PASS

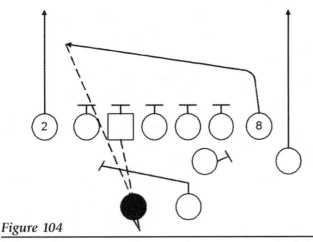

Figure 104

Figure 104 shows the most successful pass we've used after the fake of a quick kick: 8 Cross Pass. Over the years we've returned to it time and again. Our No. 8 end got loose on this play for an 82-yard touchdown in a 1959 Lawrenceville game. But that sort of thing

doesn't happen very often. More frequently we've used this play to pick up vital first downs at crucial times. In our biggest Lawrenceville game in 1970, we were behind 21-20 with a few minutes left and facing third down and 11 yards to go on our own 39-yard line. Furthermore, our first string tailback was injured and out of the game, so things looked bleak. But our sub tailback faked a quick kick and hit the No. 8 end for 13 yards and a first down. From that point we drove for the winning touchdown. A coach tends to have a warm spot in his heart for plays that bail him out of trouble.

FAKE QUICK KICK FULLBACK SCREEN

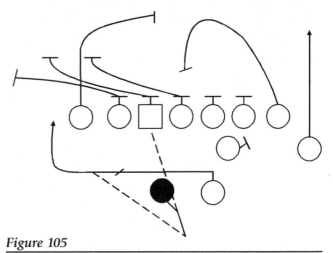

Figure 105

Fake Quick Kick Fullback Screen

Of all the screen passes we've used after faking a quick kick, the most successful has been the weakside screen to the fullback. (See Figure 105.) I've already discussed this play in the passing chapter, and it's used exactly the same way here. If anything, this version of the play is even more effective than the regular screen. If you are having success in executing any screen pass in your regular passing attack, don't hesitate to use it with a quick-kick fake. To the defense, it is a different play.

Fake Quick Kick Handback

The fake quick kick handback is a surprisingly effective play, and your players will love

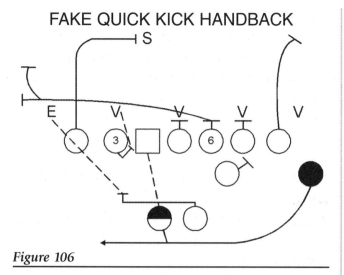

FAKE QUICK KICK HANDBACK

Figure 106

it. It is run exactly like the Statue of Liberty except for the fake kick and the handback maneuver by the tailback to the wingback. (See Figure 106.) Essentially a coach is getting two plays "for the price of one." The tailback takes his three backward steps, then moves forward and swings his kicking leg like a quick kick while at the same time swinging his arm back to hand the ball to the wing. Like his assignment on the Statue, the wing must get early depth so he can level off before accepting the ball from the tail.

We used this handback in an important 1995 Lawrenceville game for a 47-yard gain. We were using two different tailbacks that season, and the boy who executed this handback was our best quick-kicker, who had gotten off two excellent quick kicks earlier in the game. This helped set up the fake quick kick here. You must never underestimate the coaches and players across the field, but sometimes their scouting and preparation can be turned against them. If one player usually does your quick-kicking, he should be the player who executes your fake quick kick plays.

Conclusion

In this chapter I have indicated we are thoroughly sold on the value of the quick kick. In my opinion, any coach of a single wing team

should use it. Our quick kick is much easier to execute than the regular punt. It is a potent weapon that can control field position and can give you a definite psychological advantage.

The fake quick kick plays I discussed in this chapter are some we have used in games. A coach can use any play that will exploit the weakness of the opposing defense and take advantage of the strengths of his players. Whenever possible, he should use plays that are already in his offense. If he uses these plays, he'll be getting "two for the price of one" and saving valuable practice time.

Simplifying Your Kicking Game

What I will discuss briefly now is not part of the single wing offense, but I'd like to share with you some ideas about the kicking game that dovetail with our quick kick protection and coverage. In 1960 I forsook the tight punt formation for the spread punt, and I stayed with the spread punt until 1991. That season I decided to use a punt formation that was an extension of our quick kick formation. Of course, that meant we punted from our unbalanced line (right). To go one step further, I also decided to use an unbalanced line (right) for extra points and field goals. Figures 107 and 108 show these formations.

PUNT FORMATION

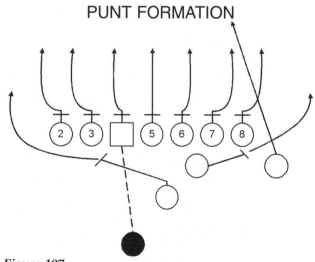

Figure 107

83

PAT FORMATION

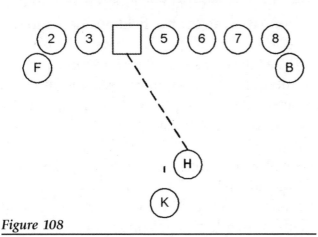

Figure 108

In the off-season I told a couple of coaches about my plan, and they said I shouldn't do it. My rejoinder was, why not? If the quick kick could give us such good protection and coverage, why not extend it to punts? And in modified form, to extra points and field goals? After using both formations for nine years, I can report they both worked very well. We have had no problems with protection, and our coverage has yielded no long punt returns. We've also been solid on extra points and have kicked more than our share of field goals. Of course, this new arrangement was no panacea: You still have to work at it. We always practiced these maneuvers *live* for a brief period every Tuesday, Wednesday, and Thursday.

Originally I had two reasons for making this change. The first was to simplify our offensive kicking game by essentially having only one kicking protection. Throughout this book I've talked about getting "two for the price of one." Now we were getting what might be considered "three for the price of one."

The second reason was to confront our opponents with two more things that were different. They already have to contend with our regular unbalanced single wing with formations right and left and variations. They already have to cope with the whole quick-kicking game. Now they have to work against unbalanced line punt and PAT formations. Being different makes problems for the defense.

High school coaches might consider trying these ideas. For the punt formation the kicker aligns with left foot on the ball 10 yards back. This is a much easier center pass than would be required from the deeper spread punt, so (for single wing centers) we've virtually eliminated the possibility of a bad snap. The assignments for all other players are identical with those on the quick kick. Again the wingback or chase man can be split out to the strongside (at A) or to the weakside (at B).

For the PAT the tee is placed directly behind the No. 5 lineman, the middle man of our formation, at 7 yards' depth. The No. 2 end moves in to split 6 inches from the next man in, just like the other linemen. At the center snap all linemen anchor their outside foot and step to the inside, staying square and using their hands. The fullback lines up splitting the outside leg of the No. 2 end, an arm's length away, and the blocking back lines up splitting the outside leg of the No. 8 end, an arm's length away. At the starting count both backs step with their inside leg to seal the inside seam, using their hands. They must protect that inside seam. That's where kicks are often blocked. For both the punt and the PAT we usually use an early or a late count. These ideas might appeal to single wing coaches who are already using the quick kick.

Chapter 8

The Use of VARIATIONS

In this chapter I will discuss the use of variations of the basic single wing formation. This is one of the strongest features of our offense. Different kinds of ends over, backfield flankers, men-in-motion, and split ends can pose real problems for a defensive team. This is particularly true at the high school level, where your opponents have often struggled to line up correctly and play effectively against the basic unbalanced line in both left and right formations. Using variations will only exacerbate their problems.

Two Key Points in Using Variations

There are two things the coach of a single wing team must keep in mind when using variations. First, the variations must not require the use of virtually new plays that demand learning additional assignments for most of your players. Instead they should be maneuvers for which most of your players can execute familiar assignments and techniques.

The second main point is to have a threat or threats in mind for each variation. You must be aware of how you can capitalize on your opponent's adjustment—or lack of adjustment—to any formation variation. During the game, the coach and his spotters must be alert to recognize adjustment weaknesses and take advantage of those weaknesses. The reader should keep these two points in mind as I discuss the variations we have used most often.

END OVER ALIGNMENT

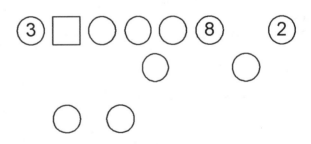

Figure 109

End Over Variation

One of the most useful of our variations is end over. In this variation the No. 2 end lines up close outside the wingback on the strongside. Figure 109 shows this alignment, which (like other variations) we use in both left and right formation. The reader will note that only the No. 3 lineman remains on the weakside of the center. Now there are five linemen on the strongside of the center. It is still a legal formation because there are seven men on the line of scrimmage. Depending on the basic play to be used, the tailback sets the alignment for himself and the fullback at far or near or close position.

END OVER PLAY NO. 49
When Defense Fails to Adjust

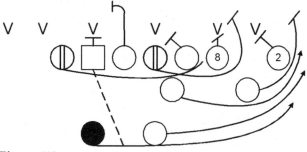

Figure 110

The Main Threat to the Defense

This simple variation can cause all kinds of problems for the defense. Now the defensive linemen must move to the strongside in some fashion to meet strength with strength. If they do not move at all, the No. 2 end will block the end man on the line to the inside, with the tailback running around end behind a mass of blocking. Figure 110 shows End Over Play No. 49 when given this advantage. This is the main threat to the defense. On a well-drilled team the end man should never be blocked in by a close flanker, but it has sometimes happened when high school players stick to their regularly assigned defensive positions against the basic unbalanced formation.

Opposing teams rarely committed such a flagrant error, but when they did, we tried to capitalize on that mistake before they adjusted. To illustrate the longevity of this threat: In the last game of the 1956 Lawrenceville season our tailback ran outside for 44 yards against that vulnerable defense, and in the final game of the 1999 season we capitalized on the same mistake for 59 yards.

END OVER PLAY NO. 49
Typical Defensive Adjustment

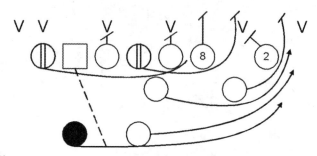

Figure 111

Typical Use of End Over Play No. 49

This sort of bonanza was rare, but we still used the play and gained good yardage with it. Here are the assignments for End Over Play No. 49. The No. 2 end should line up 2 feet outside the wingback. If he aligns wider, there is a danger of penetration ruining the play. The No. 2 end's assignment is to block the first man to the inside on or off the line. The wingback blocks any man in his inside seam because the No. 2 end usually cannot get over that far. If there is no man in his inside seam, the wing loops around the No. 2 end and blocks to the inside. This is what usually happens. Figure 111 shows this coordination between the end and the wing. All other players execute their usual Play No. 49 assignments, with the blocking back and fullback leading the tailback around end.

End Over Play No. 48

We usually concentrate our end over attack first in the off-tackle area. End Over Play No. 48 has been highly consistent. On this play we ask the No. 2 end to align 3 feet from the wing to widen the hole a bit. He is to influence any close defensive man—i.e., fake blocking him to the inside and then run downfield to block. The wing does the same

END OVER PLAY NO. 48
Typical Defensive Adjustment

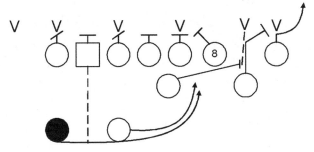

Figure 112

thing unless there is a man head-on the No. 8 end, in which case he follows his normal Play No. 48 rule and power-blocks that man. All other players execute their regular Play No. 48 assignments. (See Figure 112.)

End Over Play No. 48 is especially effective used near the goal line or going for a first down. In those situations the defense often does not adjust properly or get set on time, thus creating a porous off-tackle area.

Further End Over Attack

As we continue using the end over variation during a game, we may employ seam bucks or other inside plays to take advantage of openings in the line. If the defense overshifts too far to the strongside, we are always prepared to use a strong weakside play like End Over Play No. 21 Power.

End Over Play No. 99 Pass

The most effective pass we have used from end over is a modified version of Play No. 99, a running pass. (See Figure 113.) As the reader can see, we have maximum protection on this play with blocking by the No. 8 end (who is now an ineligible receiver), by the blocking back, and by the fullback. The primary receiver is the No. 2 end, who runs a banana pattern, but the wingback is also frequently open in the flat. This play has given us some substantial gains. In the biggest game of the 1998

Lawrenceville season, we used this pass to score our clinching touchdown.

Swap Play No. 21 Pass

There is one other related maneuver that should be mentioned here. If we have been using a lot of end over, in which there is no eligible receiver on the shortside, an effective change-up is our swap variation. At quick glance this looks like end over, with only one man to the weakside of the center, but now that *one* man is an eligible receiver, the No. 2 end. The No. 3 lineman and the No. 8 end have been moved to new places on the strongside. Figure 114 shows Swap Play No. 21 Pass, one of the passes we've used from this alignment. Except for No. 3 and No. 8, the assignments are identical with those on our regular Play No. 21 Pass. The element of surprise is what makes this change-up effective.

END OVER PLAY NO. 99 PASS

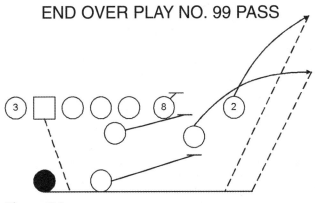

Figure 113

SWAP PLAY NO. 21 PASS

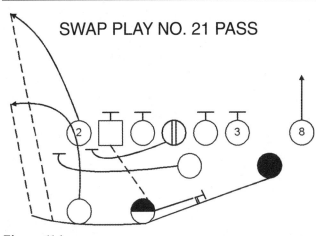

Figure 114

Fullback Weakside Variations

Our fullback weakside package has been highly effective, especially when used against overshifted defenses like the Adjusted Oklahoma (3-4) Defense. There are two closely related, but slightly different, parts to the package: the tailback and the fullback changing places (Zip), and the fullback flanked close on the weakside (3X). In each case these alignments can mount critical pressure on the defensive team to our weakside. (See Chapter 10 for a discussion of defenses used against the single wing.)

Figures 115 and 116 show these alignments. Though they look different to the opposing team, we can run many of the same plays from each one. We can also run some different plays better from each one.

The threats to the defense come from what we call "Sweep" and "Option," two compan-ion plays. Sweep is an end run to the weakside by the tailback behind powerful blocking. Option is an option run or pass to the weakside by the tailback behind strong blocking. Both these plays can be executed from either Zip or 3X. You can use the alignment that fits in better with what you're doing on offense in a game.

ZIP SWEEP

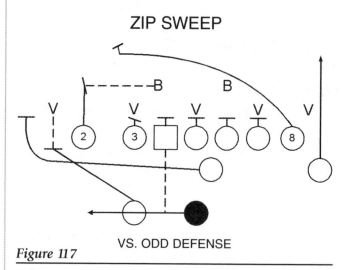

VS. ODD DEFENSE

Figure 117

Zip Sweep

Let's start with Sweep, a play used occasionally as a surprise maneuver. Figure 117 shows the play run from Zip; all blocking assignments are the same from 3X. The fullback blocks the end man on the line, the No. 2 end blocks the second most dangerous man, and the No. 3 lineman takes the third most dangerous. The blocking back lines up between the No. 5 and the No. 6 linemen and runs to the weakside as a personal interferer for the tailback, who takes a lead center and runs around end. These are the key assignments.

The strongside linemen, from the center through the No. 7, block any man on them or brace up to prevent penetration. The No. 8 end sprints across to block in the secondary. The wingback, who is sometimes split out at A or B as a decoy, runs downfield to block.

In the above diagram the tailback and fullback have switched places (in the Zip alignment), but we have sometimes run Sweep

ZIP ALIGNMENT

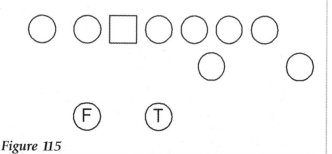

Figure 115

3X ALIGNMENT

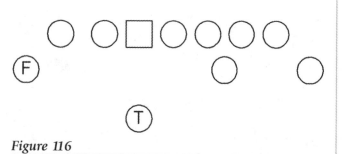

Figure 116

from regular formation if we have a fast full-back and a rugged tailback to block for him. In that case the tail will be in far position behind No. 3 and the full lined up behind No. 5. The element of surprise is greater that way, but in my experience high school players don't pick up changed backfield positions very often. From the Zip alignment we have a number of checks, such as the full running off-tackle behind the tail (Play No. 48), the tail running Play No. 24, many dropback passes, and Zip Option, which I will discuss shortly.

3X SWEEP

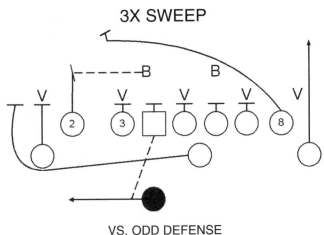

VS. ODD DEFENSE

Figure 118

3X Sweep

Figure 118 shows Sweep run from 3X. Again the fullback blocks the end man on the line, and all the other assignments are the same as on the Zip Sweep. From the 3X alignment we have a number of checks, such as Play No. 43, Fake Pass 63, Play No. 24, Play No. 21 Power, and any number of dropback passes, on which the fullback slides in to do his usual pass protection assignment. Depending on the play, the tailback will sometimes line up behind No. 5 in the usual fullback position when he is executing fullback assignments. But from the 3X alignment the best play we have is Option, which I will cover after my discussion of Q Sweep.

Q SWEEP LEFT FORMATION

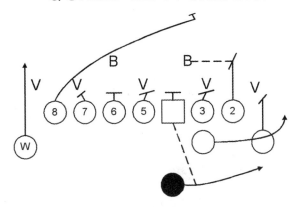

VS. ODD DEFENSE

Figure 119

Q Sweep

From either Zip or 3X we occasionally like to come out of our huddle into left formation, which is easily recognizable because of our serpentine maneuver, and run Sweep on a quick count. High school players often take too long finding their assigned positions opposite our left formation. This is most likely to happen if our opponents are using a flop-over defensive plan, in which individual players line up in the same position relative to individual offensive players, whether we are in right or left formation. When we run Sweep on a quick count, we often align the blocking back in Q position (behind the No. 3 lineman). From there he can more quickly get in front of the tailback to lead him around the weakside end—that is the right end when we're in left formation. Then we call the play "Q Sweep." (See Figure 119 for Q Sweep with 3X.)

This sort of maneuver can reap big dividends. In the 1996 Lawrenceville season we used Q Sweep at crucial points in three games, and it yielded us gains of 31, 29, and 17 yards. In the chapter on offensive planning and strategy (See Chapter 10.), I discuss measures to take against the flop-over defensive plan and other ways to use a quick count effectively.

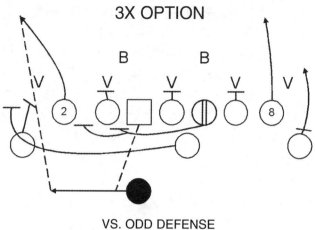

3X OPTION

VS. ODD DEFENSE

Figure 120

3X Option

Now to move to a discussion of Option, which for many years has been one of the best plays in our attack. Like Sweep, it can be executed from either 3X or Zip, but unlike its companion play, Option is not just a surprise maneuver used sparingly. Rather it's a play we have applied more frequently for large gains.

Figure 120 shows 3X Option against the Oklahoma (3-4) Defense Adjusted, which typically has the strong safely up on the strongside and a three-deep secondary. The threat of the play comes from having the fullback block the weakside end and forcing indecision on the defensive halfback: Does he come up to stop the tailback running wide behind the blocking back or does he stay back to cover the No. 2 end, who is a deep receiver?

Notice that in the diagram the No. 2 end is running a banana pattern all the way. He must *not* run downfield *first* and *then* outside. If he runs a good banana pattern, the safety cannot rotate over to pick him up, which would allow the halfback to come up quickly against the run. I call the play "Option" because our tailback has the choice of throwing deep if the halfback comes up or running if he stays back. The tailback gets a lot of practice on this play, reacting to the actions of someone simulating that halfback.

As I said in my discussion of Sweep, the coach must be alert to any adjustments the defense makes to 3X or Zip. If the defensive end widens, we can run inside him. If the weakside backer moves over, we can run a play into the area he left. If the secondary moves over, we can throw a pass into a weakened secondary area.

From 3X and Zip the assignments for all players on Option are identical. Both present the same threat to the defense, but one or the other may fit in better with what you're doing on offense in a particular game. Option is not a complicated play, but it has yielded big dividends. In the 1993 Lawrenceville season it gave us two touchdowns through the air and one on the ground. The dual threat of pass-or-run is what makes it so effective. This is especially true near the goal line. In that same 1993 season our tailback ran in a two-point play in the last minute to give us a come-from-behind victory.

The assignments for all interior linemen on Option are identical with what they are on Play No. 21 Pass, giving us "two for the price of one." The No. 3 lineman blocks the second man in on the weakside. The center blocks any man on him or (no man on) braces up. The No. 5 lineman does the same. The No. 6 lineman pulls to the weakside and checks for a blitz: first in the seam between the center and No. 3 and then close outside No. 3. The No. 7 lineman fills for the pull of No. 6. He blocks from man on No. 6 to man on him in that order. As I stressed earlier, the No. 2 end runs a banana pattern. I will cover the play of the No. 8 end and the wingback in the next section, when I discuss the other dimensions of Option.

Zip Option Middle and Option Trans

Figure 121 shows the other dimensions of this play, which are important parts of our offense. These are passes to the No. 8 end

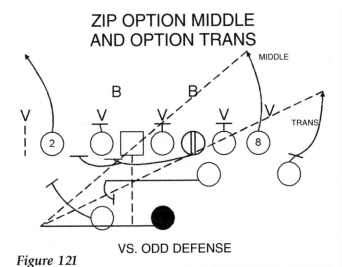

ZIP OPTION MIDDLE
AND OPTION TRANS

Figure 121

VS. ODD DEFENSE

(Option Middle) and to the wingback (Option Trans) when the tailback pulls up to throw. To execute this maneuver we set up in the Zip alignment as shown in the diagram, with the tailback behind No. 5. This position allows him to take a lead center and run under control to the weakside for four steps before pulling up and getting on balance to throw.

Starting from behind No. 3, the fullback takes a few short steps before pulling up to pass-protect. The blocking back starts from his regular position and runs over past the center to pivot around to pass-protect. The initial actions of these three backs establish flow, which is an important element of the play. All linemen have their regular Option blocking assignments, but they must be conscious of the spot from which the tailback is throwing and adjust accordingly.

The No. 8 end runs a post pattern from the start, but the wing's technique is different. He hesitates for a few counts, faking a pass protection block. Then he runs the trans pattern that is shown in the diagram. Although we have thrown these passes from both right and left formation, for a right-handed passer it is easier from left formation, running to his right. We like to throw the pass into the narrow side of the field, especially on Option Trans. We

designate which pass it is to be beforehand because we don't want the tailback looking for one receiver or the other after he sets up. Option Middle has given us a number of good gains, and Option Trans has been a real game-breaker.

We first used Option Trans in a Lawrenceville game in 1969, when it went for a 66-yard touchdown, the key play in a 21-20 victory. Since that time we have used it at crucial points in games, and it has given us some big plays. In the 1992 Lawrenceville season it yielded touchdowns in three games: for 43 and 26 yards from left formation and for 73 yards from right formation. High school defensive backs can lose track of a delayed receiver suddenly running down the sideline.

Wide Receiver Variations

There are four wide-receiver variations in our offense: the No. 8 end split wide outside the wingback to the strongside, which we call "Slot"; the wingback split out wide to the strongside, which we designate as "A"; the wingback split out wide to the weakside, which we refer to as "B"; and the No. 2 end split out wide on the weakside, which we term "Split." Each of these variations can be set up in both right and left formations.

Like other formation variations discussed in this chapter, these wide receiver variations allow us to use familiar plays that don't change the assignments of most players. Like the others, too, these variations carry a threat to the defense that the offense must be ready to exploit. In this case, the threat is a deep pass. Once this threat is established, either during a game or in previous games, we can more easily use underneath patterns and familiar running plays.

We call a deep pass to an individual wide receiver a "Go Pass." Thus we have Slot Go, A Go, B Go, and Split Go. We do not expect to throw a Go Pass very often—we may not throw one for several games—but the threat is always there. When we do throw one it will be to a fast wide receiver with good hands. The technique used on a Go Pass is the same for all four wide receivers. I will discuss this technique in the next section.

I will cover each of the wide-receiver variations in turn, mentioning the plays that go well from each one. In any game we used only a limited number of plays from one of these variations, and we practiced those plays during that week. But these simple additions to the offense can cause problems for the defense.

Slot Variation (No. 8 End Split Out)

SLOT GO PASS

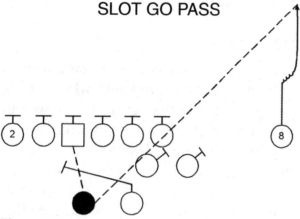

Figure 122

Slot Go Pass

Figure 122 shows Slot Go Pass. The technique used on this Go Pass is replicated by the other wide receivers on their Go patterns. The wide receiver here, the No. 8 end, must start under control downfield and to the outside and after about 15 yards turn on the speed, expecting a deep pass over his inside shoulder. When we throw this pass, we like to lull the deep secondary defender to sleep beforehand by some nonrelated plays like seam bucks, on which the No. 8 end runs downfield in lackadaisical fashion. In the opening game of our 1961 season at Wabash College, our No. 8 end followed this technique to get behind

his defender for a 54-yard touchdown. We have done the same thing a number of times since.

As indicated in the diagram, for this deep pass we want to have maximum protection, so the wingback and the No. 2 end are added blockers. They are not needed as receivers on a Go Pass because the No. 8 end is isolated on a secondary defender.

SLOT WHEEL PASS

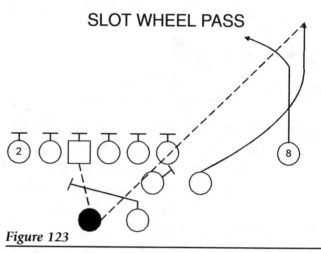

Figure 123

Slot Wheel Pass

Like other wide-receiver variations, we have two receivers to combine on a pattern. To illustrate this I will use Slot Wheel, which is pictured in Figure 123. The Wheel pattern is familiar to all students of football, so I will not go into great detail here. The idea is for the wide man, in this case the No. 8 end, to run downfield about 20 yards and bend to the inside. The inside receiver, who is the wingback here, runs to the outside fairly shallow and then turns upfield to receive a long pass over his inside shoulder. On this kind of deep two-man pattern, the other receiver can be an added blocker.

Slot 99 Choice Pass

One of the best plays we have from Slot is what I call "99 Choice Pass." The wide receiver, the No. 8 end, runs off the secondary, and the wingback runs a shallow pattern to the outside. With regular Play No. 99 blocking, the tailback takes a lead center, runs to the outside, and has the option of throwing a short

SLOT 99 CHOICE PASS

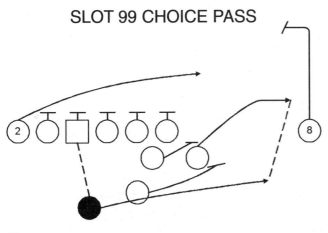

Figure 124

pass to the wingback or running with the ball, depending on the reactions of the defense. This sort of technique is familiar to the tailback from the many run-or-pass option plays in our attack. (See Figure 124.)

Other Plays from Slot

From our slot formation we have a number of plays that can be run without changing the assignment for any player. Some of the most useful plays are passing threats to the weakside, such as 21 Pass, 40 Pass, or Zip Option. These plays should be effective because the secondary tends to move over to the strongside to cope with the wide threat I have mentioned.

We have our regular assortment of passes to the No. 2 end such as Pro 2, 2 Flat and Up, and Divide 2. Again, without changing any player's assignment, we can run our Statue, our Fullback Screen, our Draw, and our 63-Shovel.

We also have available any number of our regular running plays. This would include all of our seam bucks except Play No. 17. Obviously we can no longer run off-tackle either because the No. 8 end is removed. However, there are many good running plays available like Play Nos. 43, 35, 21 Power, Zip Sweep, and regular Sweep.

Variation A
(Wingback Split Out to Strongside)

A 80-2 CROSS PASS

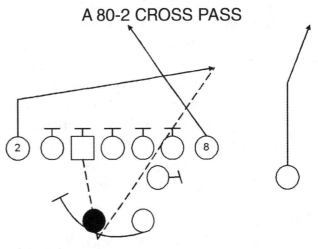

Figure 125

A 80-2 Cross Pass

The wingback split out to the strongside is our A variation. From this formation we can throw a Go Pass to the wingback or use the wingback and the No. 8 end together in a Wheel pattern or in other two-man combinations. We may also use a pass like A 80-2 Cross, which stretches the secondary and offers a wider area to connect with the crossing No. 2 end. Figure 125 shows this pattern, which we have already discussed from regular formation in Chapter 6.

Other Plays from Variation A

One of the plays we will use from A is 99 Choice, with the wingback running off the secondary and the No. 8 end running a shallow pattern to the strongside. The tailback again has the option of passing to the short receiver or running with the ball behind Play No. 99 blocking. Our favorite Play No. 99-8 Cross is also effective from this formation. (See Chapter 6 for 99-8 Cross.)

Once again we have any number of familiar running plays available in this variation. With the No. 8 end now in his regular position we can use Play Nos. 57 and 57 X, and all our seam bucks. We can also use Play Nos. 84

and 83, Fake Pass 63, the Fullback Screen, and the Draw.

By placing the wingback split out to the strongside, we hope to force the defensive secondary to compensate, opening up the weakside. Zip Option, Sweep, or Zip Sweep should go well. We also have our regular passes to our No. 2 end, such as Pro 2, 2 Flat and Up, and Divide 2. Finally, this is an excellent formation from which to quick-kick, with the wingback doing his regular job as chase man and our regular quick-kick protection intact.

Variation B
(Wingback Split Out to Weakside)

This wide-receiver variation can cause the defense problems because it is so unorthodox. By placing the wingback wide to the weakside, we should force the defense to change their secondary positions. We can still use many familiar basic plays with little or no change for our offensive players.

B CUT-OFF PASS

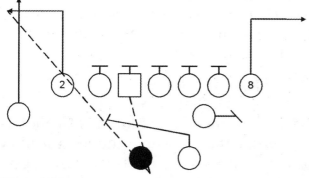

Figure 126

B Cut-Off Pass

From Variation B we have an excellent Cut-Off pattern in which the wingback runs off the secondary and the No. 2 end runs a pro pattern underneath. (See Figure 126.)

B Zip Option

We have had great success in the past with B Zip Option, on which the No. 2 end runs a shallow pattern underneath the wingback and

B ZIP OPTION

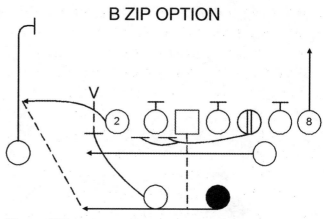

Figure 127

the tailback has the choice of throwing to him or running the ball, depending on the defensive reaction. (See Figure 127.)

PLAY NO. B 99 PASS

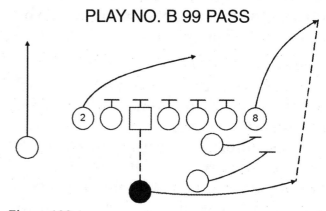

Figure 128

Play No. B 99 Pass

If the defensive secondary adjusts too far to the weakside, we can use Play No. B 99 Pass to the No. 8 end. Figure 128 shows Play No. B 99 Pass, a running pass with the No. 8 end running a banana pattern and no change in assignment for any player.

Other Plays from Variation B

We start this discussion with the familiar patterns of the Go Pass and the Wheel Pass, in which the wingback and the No. 2 end coordinate to run the pattern.

For running plays we can use all of our seam bucks and attack the off-tackle area with Play Nos. 57 and 57 X. We can also use Play

Nos. 84, 83, Fake Pass 63, and the Draw, Fake Pass 64, and Delay 8.

Lastly, variation B is a good formation from which to quick-kick. The wingback, split wide, is in an excellent position to do his regular chase man assignment, and there is no change in our kick protection.

Split Variation
(The No. 2 End Split Out)

On the Split Variation there is no change in our whole strongside attack. From this formation we can use our seam bucks, our off-tackle plays, our end run, and our running passes. We can also use the Draw, the Fullback Screen, and many passes.

On the weakside we start with the Go Pass to the No. 2 end. We can also run a good Sweep, Zip Sweep, or Play No. 21 Power behind the No. 2 end, who has run off the secondary support.

SPLIT PLAY NO. 21 PASS

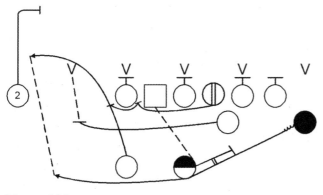

Figure 129

Split Play No. 21 Pass

Of all our weakside plays, the most successful has been Play No. 21 Pass, with the split No. 2 end running off the secondary and the tailback taking his usual route in the weakside flat. The wingback has the choice of passing to the tailback or keeping the ball and running, depending on the reactions of the defense. Figure 129 shows Split Play No. 21 Pass.

Conclusion

Variations of the basic single wing formation can cause severe problems for your opponent. If the other team has not prepared in advance for a formation variation, it can be hard for their players to adjust. In a game during the 1982 Lawrenceville season, we scored a touchdown on End Over Play No. 48 and returned to it from time to time for good gains. The opposing coach, growing more and more frustrated, kept yelling to his players to "adjust." But they never did get into position to stop a basic off-tackle play run from such a simple variation. Without this play we would not have won a close game.

A well-prepared defense will not only have to adjust to each known variation but will have to be oriented to which plays might be used most effectively from each one. And for the most part these can be basic plays, calling for little change in blocking assignments. If you can force the other team to spend more time preparing for a formation variation than you spend installing it, you have gained a clear advantage.

This flexibility of the offense helps to limit the number of defenses and defensive stunts that an opponent will have time to prepare for you. In my opinion, it is wise to have several methods of varying your formation ready for each game, though from each variation you may use only a few plays. This can force your opponent to limit himself to one basic defense and to a few stunts, giving your offense a distinct edge.

Chapter 9

PREPARING
for a Season

We play football games in the fall, but a conscientious coach involves himself with the sport all year long. In this chapter I will guide the reader through the planning and activities that would occupy a typical high school single wing coach from the close of one season to a point where he can set up the game plan for the first game of the next season. Many of the topics I'll cover would be applicable to any offensive system, but some of them are particularly relevant to the single wing offense.

Among other things, I will discuss such subjects as getting maximum benefit from movies, compiling and utilizing an offense notebook, providing for informal single wing practices, deciding what to teach first when installing this offense, making practices more productive, and setting up a helpful game plan. A coach has many things to do in preparation for a season.

Preliminary Planning and Activities

In December the coach should set up a weight-training program for all returning players. When to begin would vary with the school,

but once you start, there should be regular attendance under adult supervision. Obviously the head coach should be present much of the time.

Early on, the coach should meet with his team doctor and trainer to discuss potential injury procedures. He should also foster good relations with his booster club and try to get any needed equipment.

Planning for Informal Practice

Depending on the school situation, the coach should make plans for a time period, probably in the late spring, when he can have noncontact practice sessions with at least some of his players. Included in this group would be centers, passers, receivers, and potential quick-kickers, if you are going to use that weapon.

Enough cannot be said about the importance of the center, who is the key to any single wing attack. You will not have an effective offense if this player is not accurate on the various types of center passes that are used. (See Chapter 3 for teaching this position.) You must plan on having enough centers for both varsity and jayvee teams. And these boys must be trained before you run plays as a team. If you can't arrange to work with players at any other position, you must at least do some advance work with your centers so they can practice productively on their own over the summer.

Potential tailbacks and wingbacks should work on the "across the field drill," and tailbacks should get used to taking a direct center pass before running with the ball or setting up to throw a dropback pass. They should get started throwing various types of passes to the ends and wingbacks. Wingbacks should practice throwing reverse passes. (See Chapter 6.) Fullbacks should work on learning the half spin or the full spin. (See Chapters 3 and 5.) Blocking backs should practice huddle procedure and calling cadence. If circumstances permit, linemen should be included to practice stance, starts, and pulling. (See Chapter 3.)

Planning to Improve Game Movies

One of the important areas many high school coaches could improve is game movies. Too many schools take their movies from low elevation so you can't see what's going on in the interior line and can't study defensive spacing. By building a platform on low stands, erecting a tower, or using a forklift, the coach could get increased elevation for more useful movies. The time to plan for any such improvement is well before the season starts.

Other ways you could improve movies during games would be to record down-and-distance and take a shot of the scoreboard after every score. Too many photographers don't start the film early enough before the play begins or continue taking pictures a few more seconds after the play ends so you can better locate the players you're tracking. In the days of 16 mm film, expense was a factor, but now

with camcorders these measures can be taken inexpensively.

Other Uses of Films

With regard to movies, a coach should make up training films that can be used in out-of-season staff discussions and in teaching the offense during preseason practice. And highlight films are wonderful ways to spark enthusiasm in the off-season among players and boosters.

If a coach is putting in the offense for the first time, he should make sure to show his players films of a good single wing team as soon as possible. There is no better way to sell players—and assistant coaches—on a new offense. Later in this chapter I will offer some suggestions to the high school coach who is installing the single wing as a new offense.

Compiling an Offensive Notebook

Some time before preseason practice begins, the head coach should compile a well-organized offensive notebook that can be used by all coaches and players. This notebook can serve both as a teaching aid during early practice and as a source of reference later on. It should contain diagrams of all basic plays and variations, and information about the signal system.

Before the players see this notebook, the coaching staff should go through it play by play, discussing each page with the aid of movie analysis as illustration where needed. The head coach should use a stop-and-go projector in his analysis. This discussion should cover the techniques used on plays and information about when certain plays are best utilized. The entire staff must be "on the same page."

The Depth Chart

The next important task is making up an offensive depth chart, which often provokes considerable discussion among the coaches as to where boys should be placed. We try to select players for the different positions who are best fitted to do the jobs we will ask of them. But this is not easy. Sometimes we guess wrong as to a player's capabilities, and sometimes we have to move him to a position where there has been an injury to the boy playing there. Ideally we will place a boy in a suitable spot from his first day of practice as a jayvee until he is a senior so he can learn as much as possible about playing that position.

The situation at schools varies, but at Lawrenceville, with a combined varsity and jayvee squad of 70 plus, we ended up with six or seven boys at a position. The top three or so would be varsity players, and the bottom three or four would be jayvees. We usually would split up into varsity and jayvee groups during part of each practice, and during the season the jayvees would play a separate schedule of games on Mondays, but throughout preseason practice the jayvee boys would cover much the same ground as the older varsity players.

In making up our depth chart, we tried to have quality substitutes or "swing men" available at key positions: The second string center might be starting at No. 3 or No. 5, but he would also practice some at center, thus giving us insurance at that critical position. We also tried to have insurance at the other key interior line positions, No. 6 and No. 7.

In like manner, the starting wingback might get some work at tailback if he was a better player than the sub tailback. In the best of all possible worlds the coach would have quality players two and three deep at every position, but that does not happen very often. In the meantime, the high school coach often must provide special insurance against injury at two or three positions.

Planning Preseason Practices

The coach must plan his overall preseason practice in advance: what offense (or defense or kicking) he will introduce in each of the double sessions. I strongly recommend that the coach have a pre-practice meeting before each session of double practice so once the squad runs on the field, there will be a concentration on individual drills and team maneuvers and a minimum of lecturing.

Time is always the enemy of the football coach. There is only a limited amount of teaching time, and it must be used productively. The head coach must set up a practice schedule that accounts for every minute. If an assistant coach has 20 minutes to work with interior linemen on blocking techniques, he should have his boys rotating on the sled or bags, not listening to a lengthy discussion of the theory of blocking. What is needed is a quick explanation and demonstration of what is to be done and then have the boys do it as often as possible. During the season, time is even more valuable when practice hours are reduced, and there are no pre-practice meetings.

With a little planning, you can often get more done in hot weather if you have players go out in shorts, shoulder pads, and helmets for one of your double workouts. This is when you're well along, not in the beginning when most states mandate having the boys start with only shorts and T-shirts.

After the squad has had a good bit of contact work in drills and when you have enough plays ready, you will want to have some controlled intrasquad scrimmages. Once the season begins, we have few scrimmages, preferring to go "thud" instead. But football is a contact game, and you have to build up to hitting. If you have a controlled scrimmage during the last portion of a practice, that is the best way. If you scrimmage in the beginning, you won't get much accomplished during the last part of a practice.

You have to plan a scrimmage in advance: who's on offense and who's on defense, the plays to be run, and against what defensive spacing. If you have enough coaches, the jayvees can be scrimmaging at the other end of the field. At this point there should be no attempt to register downs and distance, and no boy should scrimmage too long.

What to Teach First

A good question is which plays to introduce and teach first. The answer is: Be guided by common sense. Basic plays that have the three different ball carriers running with the ball should be introduced as soon as possible from both right and left formation. To save time, these plays should be run off the strip from a skeleton backfield first while the linemen are learning their assignments and working on fundamentals.

First, teach running plays that you will be using frequently: e.g., the off-tackle play (Play No. 48) for the tailback, a seam buck like Play No. 16 for the fullback, and the inside reverse (Play No. 43) for the wingback. (See Chapter 4.) In a pre-practice meeting the coach should diagram these plays on a blackboard, and he should also show them on training film as soon as possible. The players should refer to their notebooks during meetings. The game is an intellectual challenge as well as a physical challenge.

Common sense suggests that the end run (Play No. 49) should be added early. (See Chapter 4.) So should Play No. 24, if you are using the fullback half spin, or Play No. 34, if you are using the fullback full spin. (See Chapter 5.) Seam bucks are the easiest running plays to add. Using them, you can attack anywhere

in the interior. I would also add the outside reverse (Play No. 21 Power) for the wingback. (See Chapter 4.)

To get started with the passing offense, you need a dropback pass like Divide, running passes (Play Nos. 79 and 99), and reverse passes (Play Nos. 40 Pass and 21 Pass). These plays should be practiced by the backs and ends from both right and left formations on the strip before including all the linemen. I would add the Statue to the passing attack. It's easy to teach and is a good fake-pass play. It's also a maneuver your players will enjoy using. These plays are discussed in Chapter 6.

Because the quick kick is crucial in our offensive philosophy, we always introduced it on the first day of practice. (See Chapter 7.) If you want your players to think something is important, let it be "front and center." (The same thing goes for the punt.) Along with wind sprints, at the end of practice the players can do a lot of running, fanning out, and covering quick kicks and punts.

Finally, I would teach two formation variations: the end over and a weakside fullback variation, either Zip or 3X. These variations are easy to teach and pose problems for the defense. (See Chapter 8.)

Using the Offense for the First Time

If your team is using the single wing for the first time, you would follow the general procedure I have outlined above, but go more slowly. You must make sure the centers can make accurate passes to the tailbacks and fullbacks before you run plays as a team. Even though you and the team are anxious to introduce many plays quickly, go slowly.

Make sure each boy can take a proper stance. Make sure you have efficient, smooth huddle procedures. Make sure the blocking back calls signals with authority, and the team breaks from the huddle with precision and runs to the line with enthusiasm. Make sure your players are lined up correctly, and insist they get off on the count. In Chapter 2 I have outlined our numbering system, huddle procedure, and cadence, but there are any number of other ways to do it. Just do it with authority and discipline.

An inexperienced team will not have as many plays as a veteran group, but you should take solace from the fact that you don't need as many. If this is your first year with the offense, there is probably not one opposing player who has ever seen the single wing, let alone played against it. And I venture this would usually go for opposing coaches as well. They will not defense you intelligently in the beginning. You don't need a proliferation of plays; what you need is a small number you can execute efficiently.

If I were introducing the single wing offense to a high school team, I would aim to have the following plays installed by the first game: the off-tackle (Play No. 48), the end run (Play No. 49), the inside reverse (Play No. 43), the outside reverse (Play No. 21 Power), enough seam bucks to hit any opening in the interior line, and the wedge. (See Chapter 4.) The wedge would be run from right formation only; everything else, from both left and right formations.

For an aerial attack, I would have ready (from both left and right formations) a couple of dropback passes, the basic running pass (Play No. 79), and one of the reverse passes (40 Pass or 21 Pass).

I would not have any indirect attack plays ready yet. The 4 hole (Play Nos. 24, 34, and 84) is one of the best maneuvers in our whole offense, but it is probably our most sophisticated play and takes time to teach. As the season went on, I would add some indirect plays from either the 20 or the 30 series, with emphasis on the 4 hole. (See Chapter 5.)

The last two things I'd have ready for the opening game would be the quick kick and the end over variation. (See Chapters 7 and 8.) These two maneuvers are easy to install and can cause real problems for the defense. For the second or third game I'd add a weakside fullback variation, either Zip or 3X. (See Chapter 8.)

Outside Scrimmages

Near the end of your preseason practice, you should schedule at least two scrimmages with other schools. Ideally the first encounter would be a controlled teaching scrimmage. Coaches would be on the field to correct mistakes (quickly, I hope), and all coaches for both schools would stay behind the offensive team. Without regard to down and distance, each team would run, say, 12 plays, then repeat the process. The coaches would let their opponents know when they were using younger boys. There would be officials on the field to point out infractions.

Ideally the final scrimmage would be scheduled for the Saturday before your opening game. This would be a full-scale game except for live kick-offs and punts, with each team wearing game uniforms, officials on the field, and down-and-distance registered. It is essential that you take movies of at least your final scrimmage with an accompanying record of each offensive and defensive play, just as you do in regular games.

Getting the Most Benefit from Your Films

To get the most out of game films, I believe a coach should have an organized plan. At Lawrenceville we had film comment sheets that were used to record information during the game so in their analysis the next day the coaches could easily locate each play. (See Figure 130.)

FILM COMMENT SHEET

Play No.	Dn. & Dist.	Field Posit.	Formation & Play	Defense	Gain	Comments

Figure 130

On these sheets for each play (numbered consecutively in the far left column) there are spaces for the down and distance, the field position, the formation and play: e.g., L 49 or R 48 (standing for Left formation, Play No. 49 or Right Formation, Play No. 48), the defense (optional), the gain or loss (+ or –), and necessary comments on individual players. As the game unfolded, someone on our sideline would jot down this information on one of these sheets attached to a clipboard. If you choose, the gain or loss on the play can be recorded exactly by the coaches during their analysis on Sunday along with their comments on player performances.

High schools vary in the responsibilities of their assistant coaches, but someone must analyze the game film to comment on the good play and mistakes of individual players. Once you're into the season, if the whole staff is involved, it may take no more than three hours. If the head coach is doing it alone with the help of his stop-and-go projector, it will take much longer; but the upcoming movie session is the most important teaching period of the week, and the coach must be thoroughly prepared. Anyone who takes only a cursory look at the film before showing it cannot do a good job of teaching.

The Squad Film Session

When we had our squad film session on Monday afternoon, all our coaches would be present. Here was our procedure. Looking at the comment sheets, one coach would call out each play in advance: e.g., "Right 48" or "Left 21 pass." (This stands for Play No. 48 or Play No. 21 Pass. Coaches and players didn't use a Play No. in conversation.) I would show the play once and run it back, then the assistant coach would call out the comments written on his sheet one after the other (e.g., "blocking back get a better scoop when you trap" or "tailback run straight downfield") while I ran the play back and forth. Occasionally I would stop the projector and draw a necessary diagram on the blackboard. During the week, position coaches would work with individual kids to correct the mistakes that showed up in the film.

The Game Plan

We come now to the offensive game plan for the first game. Actually I never used that term. No matter how complex the game plan may be for major colleges and professional teams, it should not be an arcane document for high school teams. We intended to use in a game only what we had practiced during the week. I can seldom remember using anything else.

The game plan, as such, was divided into four parts on a sheet of paper I carried with me on a clipboard during games. The first part was nothing more than an offense depth chart, listing all players by position who dressed for the game. Occasionally I would circle the name of a boy in red ink, especially if he was a "swing man," a player not normally at that position.

Next I would list all plays that might be used, set up from strongside to weakside. This listing helped me visualize where we might attack once we saw what our opponents were doing defensively.

The third part would be plays listed by categories: e.g., short yardage plays; long yardage plays; variations, and what plays should be used with each variation; 2 point PAT plays; fake quick kick plays; blocking back false key plays. None of these plays would be new; we would have practiced them during the week. In the next chapter I will list the plays I might include in each category.

The fourth part was points to remember. There would be no more than five or six of them. I will list five points here to illustrate what this type of thing might be like. In each case I will state the point and then in parentheses beneath it explain why I emphasized that point.

Points to Remember

1. **Use action passes on first down: e.g., 40 Pass, 21 Pass, 99-8 Cross, 79, 30-Ends Cross.**
   (In last year's game we ran the ball on almost every first down.)

2. **Use fake quick kick Divide Wing.**
   (In the past, in every quick kick situation they have instructed their safety to play deeper and then sprint backward at the first indication of the tailback's runback before quick-kicking.)

3. **Use End Over Sweep or Zip Sweep**
   (Teams are defending our end over with an extreme overshift. From end over we have not run anything to the weakside for some time.)

4. **Use variation B plays: e.g., B 84, B Go, B Zip Option, B 81, B 99.**
   (We have not used the B variation against them for several years, and they may not defense it well.)

5. **Get the ball to Jim Jones: 40 Pass, 21 Pass (deep), Zip or 3X Option, Pro 2, Pro 2 and up, and 30-Ends Cross.**
   (At No. 2 End, Jim has the speed and hands to exploit their slow defensive halfbacks.)

Conclusion

I hope this discussion has been helpful to high school single wing coaches. In the off-season you do many of the things that other football coaches do, but you also have some special tasks that are concerned with using a different style of offense.

In this chapter I have taken the reader through the planning and activities that would occupy a typical high school single wing coach from the end of one season to the beginning of the next season in September. I have covered subjects I think are essential to the success of a program: utilizing an offense notebook, setting up a weight-training program, providing for informal single wing practices, deciding what to teach first, having productive practices, getting the most from your movies, and setting up a game plan. These are some of the many jobs that face a single wing coach in preparing for an upcoming season. In the next chapter I will discuss play selection and other aspects of offensive strategy.

Chapter 10

Aspects of SINGLE WING STRATEGY

In this chapter I will discuss aspects of offensive strategy a high school single wing coach will find helpful. Included are topics like attacking obvious defensive weakness, understanding categories of plays, studying traditional defenses used against the single wing, aligning players to advantage, and moving players to different positions. At the end of the chapter I will discuss the controversial topic of keying the blocking back, and diagram false key plays we have used successfully.

Attacking Obvious Defensive Weaknesses

Before discussing traditional offensive strategy, it would be wise to talk about reacting to obvious defensive weaknesses. There are two kinds of glaring defensive weaknesses: weaknesses in opposing personnel and weaknesses in the design or alignment of the opponent's defense. If the other team has shown their linemen have trouble stopping the inside running game, you should attack there from the start. If the other team's secondary players have given them a porous pass defense, you should attack them there early. You may know about such weak areas in advance from scouting or film exchange, or you may uncover them during a game. In either case you must attack them without delay.

It should not be necessary to emphasize this point, but many times coaches ignore the obvious. For example, I have seen too many instances where a team with a tall, athletic receiver waits until too late to pit that boy against a mediocre secondary player who is half a foot shorter. If you are lucky enough to encounter a mismatch, you should try to start exploiting it early in the game.

Sometimes you are completely surprised by an unorthodox defensive scheme that can turn out to be a glaring weakness. In a 1972 Lawrenceville game, the opposing coach was determined to stop our ground attack, so he set up a defense with all 11 of his players within 5 yards of the line of scrimmage. (Usually the deepest defensive man was within 3 or 4 yards.) Needless to say, we had trouble running the ball, but we were able to complete passes in areas outside and behind that packed middle. We fired away with the running pass (Play No. 79) and the running reverse pass (Play No. 21 Pass) for a total of six touchdowns between the two plays. (See Chapter 6 for a discussion of these two plays.)

Basic Categories of Plays

To get good play selection, a coach must understand the various objectives and capabilities of his offense. He must know what yield to expect from the plays he selects. A particularly good place to start, especially for an inexperienced coach, is placing plays in three categories: short yardage, long yardage, and normal yardage.

If your selection is guided by these and other categories, you can at least avoid many bad play calls. What you do select will be based on your total understanding of your offense. You may not find "the best possible play" to call, but you can at least make an intelligent choice.

Short yardage situations call for plays that can be counted on to make a yard or two when needed. Long yardage situations call for plays that have a good chance of making at least 6 yards or more. Normal yardage plays can be used in most down-and-yardage situations. They should show an average gain of at least 3 or 4 yards a try. Typical normal yardage situations are first down and 10 and second and 6 or 7.

Included in the category of short yardage choices would be the fullback wedge and standard off-tackle plays like Play No. 48 and End Over Play No. 48. We can depend on the wedge when we need a yard for a first down or a touchdown. (See Chapter 4 for a discussion of our consistent success with this play.)

The two off-tackle plays are good bets to pick up a yard or two when needed, but they are more than short yardage plays: They can also be used successfully in many normal yardage situations. I would not hesitate to use Play No. 48 on third down and six on the other team's 30-yard line, but I would not select that play on third down and six on our 30-yard line. Why? The answer is field position, a factor you must always consider.

On our end of the field or around the midfield area we are in "three down" territory (punting on fourth down), but around our opponent's 40- or 35-yard line we are going into "four down" territory. (With gains, we would not punt on fourth down.) So you must not automatically consider third down and six a long yardage situation. When we had a long yardage situation, we selected plays like Pro 2, Delay 8, Play No. 79 or Play No. 21 Pass (especially to the short receiver), Delay Wing, the Statue, or a Screen Pass. (See Chapter 6 for a discussion of these plays.)

Other Categories of Plays

A coach can set up other categories of plays to guide him. Here are a few to consider: 2 point PAT plays, "running" down action pass plays, fake quick kick plays, false key plays.

For 2 point PAT situations, we have had success with plays like 99-8 Cross, 79, and 21 Pass (Chapter 6); Zip Option and Zip Sweep (Chapter 8); and Play No. 49 and Solo (Chapter 4). For action passes used on first down or any "running" down, we have had success with 99-8 Cross, 40 Pass, 21 Pass, 79, 30-Ends Cross, and 48 Jump, among others (Chapter 6). Fake quick kick plays that have been successful are Divide Wing, 8 Cross, Play No. 49, Seam Bucks, and the handback (Chapter 7). Some false key plays are discussed and diagramed in a separate section later in this chapter. That is an important subject.

Right Formation or Left Formation

From either hash mark we normally set our unbalanced line formation to the wide side of the field. Having done this, we can call end runs, off-tackle plays, or running passes to the wide side, reverses to the narrow side, and seam bucks and traps up the middle. We can also call all sorts of passes. From the middle of the field we usually end up running about two thirds of our plays from right formation. But from either right or left formation we can mount a balanced attack.

At times it's good strategy to set your formation into the narrow side of the field. Against teams that constantly overshift to the wide side, you can have success with running plays like 48, 49, and even End Over 49 into the narrow side. The gains may be short, but they can be steady. There are certain plays that go better with your offense set into the narrow side. Included in this group are the Keep and Play No. 21 Power (Chapter 4), 40 Throwback Pass (Chapter 5), and Option Trans (Chapter 8). It's a case of knowing your own offense.

Facing Many Different Defenses

Many opposing coaches are not familiar with the unbalanced line single wing and have a difficult time setting up defenses to cope with a novel formation. The result is that single wing teams can expect to face many different and unpredictable defenses. This is particularly true of opposing teams that use "gap control" defenses; a defensive lineman playing in a 4-4 or 4-3 scheme who is used to aligning inside shade or outside shade on an offensive lineman and controlling a gap, may be asked to play head-up on a single wing lineman. It is a bit easier for Oklahoma type defensive teams (today often called "3-4 defensive line teams"). But they, too, must make some adjustments. The fact that single wing teams line up in both right and left formation makes it doubly difficult.

Role of the Spotter

Since a single wing team can expect such a diversity of defenses today, it is crucial for the coach and his spotters to pick up defensive alignments. As a coach on the sidelines, from time to time I would move downfield as far as possible to get an idea of how the defense was lined up. But the spotters, observing from a higher position, can see the defensive front better, and over the headphones they must pass on this information as precisely as possible to a coach writing down defensive positions.

When the game begins, we usually don't want the spotter to start suggesting plays that will work. That can come later. What we want is concise, accurate information about the prevailing defensive alignment: e.g., "They have a man head-on No. 5 and men on the outside shoulder of No. 7 and No. 3," or "They have a man head-on the wingback," or "Their backers are head-on the center and on No. 6 and up close."

With the other team's problems in teaching a new defense in only one week of practice time, there are often open areas in the defensive line. Seam bucks are ideal for striking at such areas. These plays may not yield large gains, but they can keep a drive going. And seam bucks are easy plays to run effectively from both right and left formations. (See Chapter 4.)

From his elevated position, the spotter can make many important observations. He may note that our opponent is consistently overshifting to the wide side from the hash mark, regardless of how we set our formation. Or he may pick up tendencies to stunt backers on certain downs. Or, knowing a false key play is coming, he may see whether linebackers are keying the blocking back. Or he can quickly observe what defensive adjustments the other team makes to our flanker and end over variations.

Traditional Defenses Used Against the Single Wing

Before I discuss how we attack common defensive arrangements, it would be helpful to look at traditional defenses used against the unbalanced line single wing. In the era just before World War II, when the single wing in one form or another was the most widely used formation, there was a consensus that to stop this attack you needed an eight front alignment of some kind. This is still true today, and coaches should keep it in mind. If your opponents do not have eight men on or close to the line of scrimmage, with force men on the outside, they will not be able to stop your running attack or optional running passes to the outside.

The most common defenses were six man lines, the 6-2 normal, the 6-2 overshift and the 6-2 undershift. Along with these defenses, coaches also used some form of the 5-3, especially against passing attacks. The secondary was, of course, a three-deep zone or man-to-man, usually a zone. For short yardage most coaches used a 7-1 (the 7 diamond) or 7-2 (the 7 box).

the four interior linemen in the seams between two offensive linemen, these men could be doubleteamed in either direction. Seam bucks were therefore highly effective. In the later 6-2 alignments, the interior defensive men were aligned head-up with offensive linemen and could be doubleteamed in only one direction. Concurrent with this was the development of the concept of pursuit that is so important in football today: "Strike a blow on your man and run to the ball" and "Penetration cuts down on pursuit." These are familiar axioms.

The terms 6-2 overshift and 6-2 undershift came from the spacing of the six linemen as they were set up in a coordinated alignment either toward the strongside or toward the weakside of the unbalanced formation, with the linebackers compensating in the opposite direction. In one form or another (with modifications and stunts), these were the most popular defenses used against single wing teams at that time. By examining the strengths and weaknesses of these traditional defenses, a single wing coach can learn a lot about attacking the defensive alignments he may encounter today.

6-2 NORMAL DEFENSE

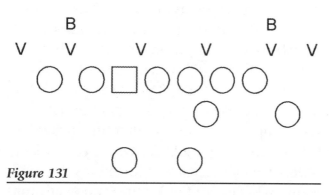

Figure 131

It is helpful to look at the 6-2 normal defense, the alignment from which the other 6-2 defenses evolved. (See Figure 131.) There were good reasons why the other two alignments superseded the 6 normal. In the 6 normal, with

6-2 OVERSHIFT DEFENSE

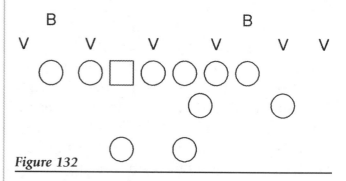

Figure 132

The 6-2 Overshift Defense

Let's begin with a cursory look at the 6-2 overshift in its purest form. (See Figure 132.) This defense was strong against the outside running attack, especially the end run (our Play No. 49) and the off-tackle play (our Play No.

48), when coaches used to insist on having the wingback power the man on him to the inside on the off-tackle play. It was vulnerable to reverses and to inside seam bucks (like our 13 and 16), and weak against inside plays like our 4-hole trap. (See Chapter 5.) With no man up close on them, the ends could release unimpeded on dropback passes. It was also hard for the strong backer to cover the flat on a running pass. In my opinion, the 6-2 overshift remained popular because it could combat the outside striking power of the single wing offense of that day.

ADJUSTED OKLAHOMA (3-4) DEFENSE

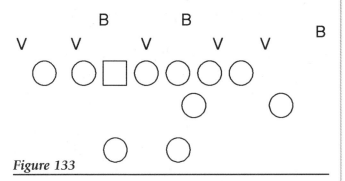

Figure 133

Adjusted Oklahoma (3-4) Defense

What often happens with this type of overshifted or odd defense today is that the backers move closer to the middle as in the Oklahoma adjusted, now often called the "3-4 defense." (See Figure 133.) This leaves the defense vulnerable to inside and outside reverses (Play Nos. 43 and 21 Power), direct runs to the weakside, and the strongside Off-Tackle play (Play No. 48) with the No. 8 end power blocking. There is now no one hindering the ends on their release for dropback passes, and the defense is weak against both the running pass (Play No. 79) and the running reverse pass (Play No. 21 Pass). These are some of the areas a single wing coach might exploit.

Overall the Oklahoma (3-4) defense is a sound scheme to use against our type of attack. It can be easily adjusted against the unbalanced line single wing offense by moving the nose man head-up on our No. 5 and aligning the strong safety outside on the strongside with a three-deep secondary. For teams normally using that style of defense against T attacks, it is an easy transition.

6-2 UNDERSHIFT DEFENSE

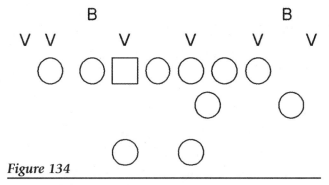

Figure 134

The 6-2 Undershift Defense

Let's look at the old 6-2 undershift, another sound defense against the traditional single wing. (See Figure 134.) When I started coaching in the fifties, it was my favorite defense against an occasional single wing opponent. It is instructive to examine this defense because we have not faced it in many years; and if a single wing team encountered it today, it could cause problems.

In its purest form the undershift was strong in many areas. Two big tackles played head-up on the ends, impeding their release on passes. A linebacker was positioned head-up on the wingback and keying him. Often this backer lined up very close to the line of scrimmage. If the wing blocked in on the tackle, the backer immediately filled the off-tackle hole. If the wing released downfield, the backer would chug him. If the wing released outside, the backer immediately went to the flat.

This defense was strong against reverses and adequate against inside fullback bucks. It was adequate but not as strong as the overshift against the end run. Of course, the defensive team also used some change-ups and stunts, but these were the most important features of the old 6-2 undershift.

Attacking a "New" Defense

It would be instructive to discuss how a single wing coach might go about attacking this defense because it is now an unfamiliar alignment. I'd begin by punching the middle with fullback seam bucks, especially 15 and 17. I'd also pound inside tackle on Play No. 57, a potent play with both the blocking back and fullback leading the tailback into the hole. (These three plays are discussed in Chapter 4.)

If the strong backer moved inside to align in front of No. 7 (becoming the wide tackle 6), I'd attack outside with the off-tackle (Play No. 48) and the end run (Play No. 49). Many single wing coaches no longer drill their wingbacks on power blocking, so it might be a problem for some teams to run an off-tackle play effectively here.

With the strong backer inside, the running pass to the blocking back in the flat (Play No. 79) would be excellent. Finally, the fullback could also exploit this defense with the 4-hole trap, which is at its best against what we refer to as an even defensive alignment: i.e., men head-up on our center and No. 6 lineman.

This would be a good time to remind the reader of the importance of variations in offensive strategy. When you are facing a tough defense, you can often get things rolling by using a variation of the basic single wing formation.

In attacking the 6-2 undershift, you could cause problems for the defense by using the end over variation, setting the No. 2 end as a close flanker outside the wingback. This would undoubtedly widen the defensive end, making for a larger off-tackle hole. If that end did not widen, our No. 2 end could block him to the inside, allowing us to use a powerful end

run (Play No. 49), with the blocking back, the fullback, and the No. 6 lineman in front of the tailback. The other team would soon have to make adjustments that might leave a weakened defensive area and cause their players to align in new and unfamiliar positions. (I discuss the use of the end over and other variations in more detail in Chapter 8.)

I hope this discussion will illustrate how a coach might go about attacking an unfamiliar defensive alignment. You may never face a 6-2 undershift, but you will encounter any number of defenses you have never seen before.

Stay With What's Successful

I believe most teams actually win games with a surprisingly small number of plays, often as few as six to eight. They may use many more plays than that during a game, but in the final analysis the plays that are really decisive in any game turn out to be few in number. Depending on your personnel and the defenses used against you, these plays will naturally vary from game to game, but some of them always seem to be the ones you count on. An intelligent coach will not forget which plays they are.

In 1973 we won a game 38-26. We scored in a variety of ways: a running reverse pass (Play No. 21 Pass), a variation of the running pass (Play No. 99-Switch), a 4-hole trap with the tailback carrying (Play No. 84), twice on the off-tackle play (Play No. 48), and a field goal. We also made substantial gains on the inside reverse (Play No. 43) and the basic running pass (Play No. 79).

Obviously these plays were telling, but what really won the game for us was the way we were able to make short, steady gains on the off-tackle play (Play No. 48). We could not stop our opponent's offense very well, but we were able to keep their offense off the field much of the time by long drives featuring the off-tackle play. We ran this play 21 times in all that day without a loss, 12 times in right formation and 9 times in left formation. We scored two short touchdowns with the off-tackle play (one from each formation), but we probably could have made those touchdowns in other ways. The effectiveness of that one play on long drives made for a classic example of ball control.

I would not want to minimize the importance of the passing game. You can't succeed with a one-dimensional offense. But there are times when you must be able to run the ball. To quote a time-worn axiom: "You pass for the show, but you run for the dough."

Aligning Your Players to Advantage

One of the ways you can help your offense is aligning some players in positions slightly different from normal. By shading players a foot or two one way or the other on certain plays, you can make it easier for them to carry out their assignments. As long as you have checks on these plays, aligning the shaded players in the same position on completely different plays, there is no giveaway. It is doubtful that high school players or their coaches, who see your offense only once a year, will recognize such changes in alignment anyway.

Here are three examples, each of which is discussed earlier in the book. If the wingback is positioned deeper on the inside reverse (Play No. 43), he can more readily take a handoff from the tailback and head directly downfield into the hole. The tailback helps facilitate this exchange by lining up closer to the line of scrimmage. (See Chapter 4.) If the blocking back is up close behind the line on Play No. 24 (or any 4-hole trap), he can more easily head up into the line to get an inside angle on the man he is trapping. (See Chapter 5.) Finally, if the tailback is aligned in "close"

position (left foot on the ball) on a quick kick, he is in a position to get maximum kick protection from his teammates. (See Chapter 7.) By using these kinds of position shading on a number of other plays, you can run your offense more effectively.

Moving Players to Different Positions

One maneuver single wing coaches sometimes resist is moving players to different positions on certain plays when it is helpful. In my section on the depth chart in Chapter 9, I talked about "swing men"—that is, players at one position who are also trained to play another position. For example, if you have two powerful fullbacks, you may want to train one of them to play tailback on certain basic plays. That can give you a "Big Boy" backfield with two fullbacks working together when you are driving for a score.

In earlier parts of this book, I discussed placing a tailback who is a good passer at wingback to throw either of our reverse passes. (See Chapter 6.) And I mentioned using Zip on Play No. 21 Power, the outside reverse, so the fullback could block the end. (See Chapter 4.) As with position shading, we have checks on switching of positions, allowing us to run completely different plays with the players in their new positions.

Permanent Position Changes

In the off-season, when you have more time to plan things, you can make position changes that will give you a better team. Looking back, we often moved boys in the hope we could get our best 11 players on the field at the same time.

The most noteworthy position change I have been involved with occurred at Lawrenceville in 1991. Going into that season our tailback was an excellent passer but not a very strong runner. We did not have a really good running back on a squad that was thin in talent. So we moved our best player, a big, fast No. 7 lineman and linebacker, to the backfield, where he would alternate between tailback and fullback while continuing to play linebacker on defense. He had never carried the ball, could not pass, and certainly didn't look like a typical schoolboy tailback since he was 6' 3" and 222 pounds.

We juggled things around so both boys would usually be in the backfield at the same time. The big former No. 7 lineman scored 14 touchdowns in our nine games, some playing tailback and some fullback. He never threw a pass. The other boy passed for many long gains and eight touchdowns, sometimes from tailback, sometimes from fullback, and occasionally from wingback. He ran the ball about three times a game. We ended up with a 6-3 season, winning probably four more games than we would have if we hadn't made a position change. Like all single wing coaches, I want our tailbacks to be both runners and passers, but sometimes you have to do something different.

Sammy Baugh as a Model

The reader may not know there was one famous single wing tailback who was a great passer but seldom ran with the ball: the legendary Sammy Baugh of the Washington Redskins, who did more than any other player to popularize the passing game in pro football. For the first seven seasons of his illustrious career, the Redskins used the unbalanced line single wing with Baugh at tailback (and sometimes at fullback while someone else, a good runner, played tailback). He was a 60-minute man, a great defensive safety man, and one of the most outstanding punters and quick-kickers of all time.

The flamboyant owner of the Redskins, George Preston Marshall, was paying Baugh a record salary to pass the football, not run with it. In 11 games in 1940 he completed 111 passes for 1,347 yards and 12 touchdowns but carried the ball only 20 times for a 0.8 yard average; in 1942 (when his team won the championship) he completed 132 passes for 1,524 yards and 16 touchdowns but ran with the ball only 20 times for a 3.1-yard average. Usually Sammy Baugh passed from tailback, but sometimes he threw from the fullback position. The single wing is a flexible formation.

Vary the Starting Count

It is important to vary your starting count. If you always go on the same count, the defense can anticipate when the center will pass the ball, and you will give up one of the advantages the offense has. Our blocking back automatically varies the starting count. He calls all 20 numbers on "two," the second Hut; all 30 number plays on "three," the third Hut; and the other plays on "one," the first Hut. All quick kicks and fake quick kicks go on "three." We usually go either very early or very late on PATs, field goals, and punts. As I mentioned in Chapter 2, we use a rhythmic cadence to make the center's job easier.

A few times a game we like to go on "Down" from an up position, in which all players have their hands on their knees. The "Down" in "Team Get Down" is the usual command for each lineman to drop down to his normal three-point stance. (See Chapter 2.) Starting early on "Down" may catch a team unprepared. When we go early, we prefer an outside running play to the strongside or the weakside, or a deep pass. Going from an up position on "Down" has given us a number of substantial gains.

Exploiting the Flop-Over Defensive Plan

One maneuver we sometimes encounter is the flop-over defensive plan. In this maneuver, individual defensive players line up in the same position with regard to the strength of the offense, regardless of whether the formation is right or left. Theoretically this scheme pits the strongest defensive players opposite the strongside of the single wing offense and the less powerful players opposite the weakside of the formation.

Here's how teams execute this maneuver. While the single wing team is in the huddle, the entire 8-front of the defensive team will wait behind the line of scrimmage to see whether the offense lines up in right or left

4-4 FLOP-OVER DEFENSE
VS.
RIGHT FORMATION

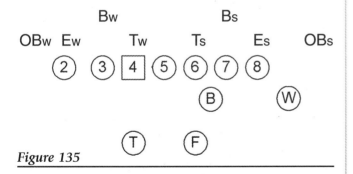

Figure 135

4-4 FLOP-OVER DEFENSE
VS.
LEFT FORMATION

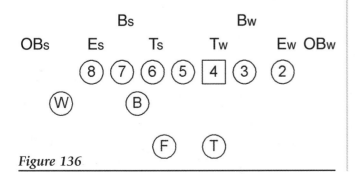

Figure 136

formation. At the first indication of this direction, the defensive signal caller yells "formation right" or "formation left," and all players move to their assigned positions. The signal caller usually takes his cue from watching where the tight end goes.

In Figures 135 and 136 we see a 4-4 defense aligned in a balanced fashion against both right and left formations. The small letters s and w in these diagrams refer to whether those players line up opposite the strongside or the weakside of the formation.

The reader can see that in both diagrams "OBs" (the strong outside backer) lines up outside the offensive wingback, "Es" (the strong end) lines up opposite the No. 8 end, "Bs" (the strong inside backer) lines up opposite the No. 7 lineman, and "Ts" (the strong tackle) lines up opposite the No. 6 lineman. So much for the strongside. In similar fashion against the weakside of these formations, "Tw" (the weak tackle) lines up opposite the offensive center, "Bw" (the weak inside backer) opposite the No. 3 lineman, "Ew" (the weak end) opposite the No. 2 end, and "OBw" (the weak outside backer) outside the No. 2 end.

For purposes of illustration here, I aligned these players head-up with offensive players, but they are often lined up in a shaded position on an offensive player or in a gap, making it more difficult to find an assigned spot in left formation. If there is confusion or tardiness in aligning defensive players, it is a good idea to go early on "Down" in left formation.

Coming out of the huddle in serpentine fashion, we indicate to the defense that we are going into left formation. They easily recognize this fact. If the complete offensive line and the wingback then line up in left formation, the defense often is not prepared for three backs lining up the other way to run 3X Sweep or Zip Sweep to the weakside, with the blocking back in Q position (behind the No. 3 lineman) leading the tailback around end. (See

Q SWEEP LEFT FORMATION

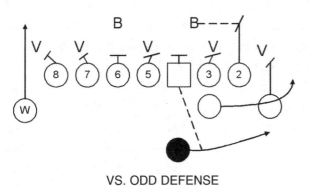

VS. ODD DEFENSE

Figure 137

Figure 137.) Then we call the play "Q Sweep." (See Chapter 8.) Because of the difficulty involved in teaching it, we seldom see the flop-over scheme at the high school level, but we continue to exploit any defenses that are slow to line up against us with plays like 3X Q Sweep or any other outside play on an early count.

Blocking Back False Key Plays

No subject in this section will be of more interest to experienced single wing coaches than blocking back false keys. For 50 years I have heard that "all you have to do to stop the single wing is follow the blocking back, who will take you to the play." That axiom is true much of the time, but it doesn't always hold up. If it did, we'd all have losing records. In fact, we would have given up using the single wing offense years ago.

Let's examine the subject. First of all, the only players who can effectively key the blocking back are the inside linebackers. If defensive linemen are standing up, looking into the backfield, they will be easy game for offensive linemen. If defensive secondary men are keying the blocking back, they will be vulnerable on many plays. Furthermore, I'm not sure high school linebackers are disciplined enough to stay with that key considering all the offensive

variations and other factors they must be aware of.

If the offense uses some false keys, plays on which the blocking back goes in a different direction, the backers will lose confidence in following him. They will see that this key is not always reliable. For that reason, a coach must make sure to have some false key plays in his offense. They can help make his attack successful.

All of the above remarks are for coaches. I seldom mentioned the subject of false keys to my players. I didn't want them worrying about football theory. I wanted them to run hard and block aggressively. Even if keying linebackers do move toward the point of attack by following the blocking back, they can still be blocked by offensive players. We always have at least one blocker in front of the ball carrier.

As a convenience to the reader, I will now diagram 10 plays we've used on which the blocking back's movement is an unreliable key. I have discussed all these plays in appropriate chapters earlier in the book.

PLAY NO. 57 X

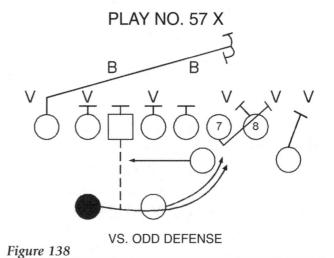

VS. ODD DEFENSE

Figure 138

Play No. 57 X

I'll start with Play No. 57 X, an off-tackle play on which the fullback leads the tailback into the hole and the blocking back runs to the weakside as a false key. (See Figure 138.) This play sometimes converts into regular Play

No. 57, with Play No. 17 blocking but with the blocking back still running to the weakside as a false key. I discuss Play Nos. 57 X and 57 in Chapter 4.

PLAY NO. 99-8 CROSS PASS

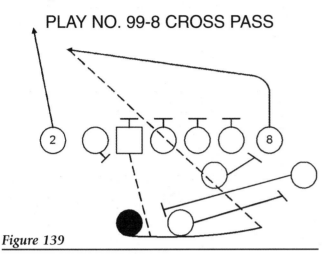

Figure 139

Play No. 99-8 Cross

The next play, 99-8 Cross, at first glance may not seem to be a false key, but it is; and the action of the blocking back has a great deal to do with the consistent success of the play over many years. As the reader can see, this is a variation of the running pass on which the tailback runs to the strongside with the ball and pulls up to hit the No. 8 end crossing over to the weakside. (See Figure 139.)

If the blocking back runs hard to block any defender in the original tight end's area, he will be a false key that jump-starts the linebackers running to the strongside. Of course, the movements of the tailback (with the ball) and the fullback add to the original draw of the blocking back, but that player's false key is vital. I discuss Play No. 99-8 Cross in detail in Chapter 6.

Play No. 35

Play No. 35 is deceptive for two reasons: the blocking back moves in a different direction from the ball as a false key, and the wingback accepts the ball close to the line of scrimmage in a well-masked maneuver so he seems to pop out of nowhere. The handoff is

PLAY NO. 35

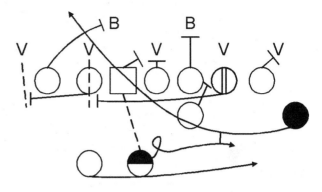

VS. ODD DEFENSE

Figure 140

so close to the line of scrimmage behind a wall of offensive linemen that it's hard to see. The No. 7 lineman pulls to trap his man, and the blocking back is a false key as he fills for No. 7. (See Figure 140.) I discuss Play No. 35 in Chapter 5.

KEEP PLAY

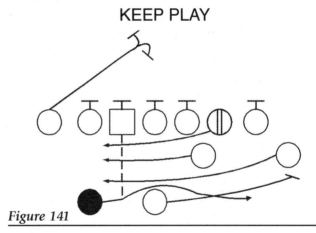

Figure 141

The Keep Play

On the strongside of the formation, the Keep Play looks exactly like Play No. 43, the inside reverse. On both plays, the blocking back runs to the weakside, the No. 7 lineman pulls to the weakside, and the wingback runs to the weakside to fake taking a handoff from the tailback. Now the tailback keeps the ball and runs around end behind the blocking fullback. (See Figure 141.) I discuss the Keep Play in Chapter 4.

KEEP PASS PLAY

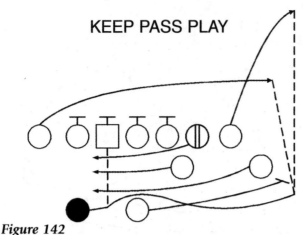

Figure 142

The Keep Pass Play

Closely related to the previous play is the Keep Pass. Like the companion play, the actions of the blocking back, the No. 7 lineman, the wingback, the tailback, and the fullback are similar to what they are on the inside reverse. Now the tailback fakes handing the ball to the wingback and passes to the No. 8 end deep or to the No. 2 end crossing over underneath. (See Figure 142.) I discuss this play in detail in Chapter 6.

PLAY NO. 48 JUMP PASS

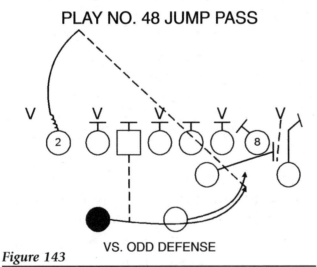

VS. ODD DEFENSE

Figure 143

48 Jump Pass Play

One of the best false keys I've ever used is Play No. 48 Jump Pass. Except for the tailback and the No. 2 end, all players execute the regular off-tackle play, and they execute it full tilt. The linemen and the blocking back block aggressively, the tailback (following the fullback)

runs an arc almost up to the line of scrimmage before jumping up and passing to the weakside end. (See Figure 143.) I discuss the details of 48 Jump Pass in Chapter 6.

PLAY NO. 12

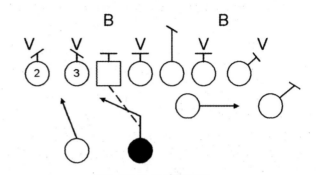

VS. ODD DEFENSE

Figure 144

Play No. 12

Play No. 12 is a member of the seam-buck family except that the fullback carries the ball behind the blocking of the tailback, *not* the blocking back. The blocking back runs to the strongside as a false key. The No. 2 end and the No. 3 lineman open a hole between them, and all linemen follow their normal seam-buck procedure of blocking the most dangerous man. (See Figure 144.) I discuss this play in Chapter 4.

PLAY NO. 99-POST PASS

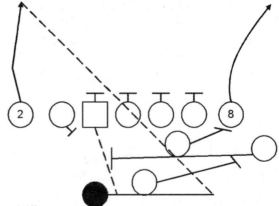

Figure 145

Play No. 99-Post

As the reader can see, this is a variation of the running pass on which the tailback stops to throw to the weakside end on a post pattern. (See Figure 145.) I cover this play in Chapter 6. Like Play No. 99-8 Cross, this is a false key pass play. The blocking back runs hard to the strongside to block any defender in the No. 8 end's original area. This action jumpstarts the linebackers moving to the strongside and out of the area where the tailback throws the pass to the No. 2 end.

PLAY NO. 21 DOUBLE REVERSE

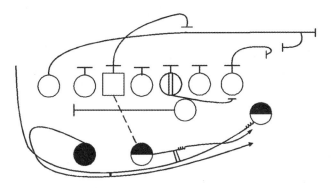

Figure 146

Play No. 21 Double Reverse

On this false key play, we have a double reverse, which I describe in detail in Chapter 5. The fullback accepts a 2 center and hands off to the wingback, who has started in quick motion, as on Play No. 21 Power. After he hands off, the full pauses unobtrusively for several seconds facing the strongside. He is waiting for the command "Go" from the tailback. As the play develops, he will block the end man on the line.

The blocking back runs to the weakside as a false key and blocks the first man he encounters. The tailback runs to the weakside before looping back to take a handoff from the wingback. When he has the ball, the tailback yells "Go" to the fullback, who runs to block the end man on the line. (See Figure 146.)

PLAY NO. 30 END AROUND

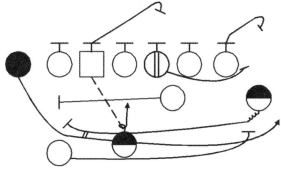

Figure 147

Play No. 30 End Around

This is an end around play off the full spin series, which I cover in detail in Chapter 5. The fullback accepts a 3 center, spins and fakes to the tailback, then gives to the wingback as on Play No. 33. The wing carries the ball over to hand to the No. 2 end, who runs around the strongside end behind the tailback's block. The blocking back is again a false key as he runs over to the weakside to block. (See Figure 147.)

These 10 plays demonstrate that the movement of the blocking back is not always a reliable indication as to where the play will go. We have used other false key plays, but these are the ones that best fit into our current offense. Other single wing coaches will have their own favorites. The important thing is to understand the purpose of these plays.

Conclusion

I hope this discussion of offensive strategy was helpful to the high school single wing coach. Offensive strategy is not some kind of exact science in which a coach can select the best possible play in any situation. But if a coach knows his own offense well enough, he can combine that knowledge with an understanding of the strengths and weaknesses of his opponent to do an intelligent job of play selection.

Chapter 11

Hail to the TEACHER-COACH

Some of the best teaching in American education today takes place on the football field. In saying this, I do not denigrate teachers of academic subjects. I have a Ph.D. in English, and I taught that subject in school and college for 54 years; so I appreciate and revere what can be done in the classroom. But many people do not understand what goes into good teaching in football, and some coaches sell themselves short. I would never do that. As a player and coach, I have known many superb teachers among football coaches.

Good teaching takes place when you bring together two elements: an able, experienced teacher who is thoroughly prepared for a particular class, and alert students who are highly motivated to learn. This is exactly what happens between coach and players in a well-organized football program.

There are certain qualities we respect in any teacher: knowledge of his subject, organized presentation of his material, enthusiasm in his presentation, fairness in all his actions, and genuine care for those he is teaching.

Some teachers have a harsher approach than others. That is often determined by their personality or their philosophy of teaching.

But, regardless of the approach, students will sense if a teacher genuinely cares about them and will respond in turn. Any good teacher will be fair and impartial in all his dealings with students. And finally there is enthusiasm. If the teacher does not really care about his subject, neither will the students. Little is ever accomplished without enthusiasm.

A teacher will accomplish a lot more by encouragement than by ridicule, particularly when working with younger students. And his tone is important. Sarcasm seldom brings about positive results. The word sarcasm is derived from a Greek word meaning to tear flesh. It is nothing more than bitter or cutting speech that wounds someone's feelings. A good teacher will avoid using it.

A conscientious football coach toils long and hard to master his complex game. Like any experienced teacher, the longer he works at his subject, the more he becomes aware of the fact that he does not know all the answers. So he usually works at it year-round.

A high school coach packs in as much football as possible during the off-season. This involves attending clinics, observing spring practice at colleges, and frequently discussing football with other coaches. Finally, it means long hours analyzing movies and studying articles and books about the game.

Each summer a high school coach works hard to evaluate his squad's recent performance. He will agonize over the game films of the previous season and assess the strengths and weaknesses of each of his own players. For better or worse, they are the only players he will have to work with that season, so he had better strive to place each boy in the best possible offensive and defensive position.

Once preseason practice begins, with two-a-day sessions, the coach's "classrooms" are in operation. From then until the season's end, a teacher of football must work at maximum efficiency, putting his students through a highly intensive course of instruction. On the practice field each minute is planned to cover the material of the course.

It is essential to work in small groups as often as possible so each boy can get individual attention from the assistant coach teaching his position. Like other classrooms, you try to make the student-teacher ratio as small as possible.

The squad movie session on Monday afternoon is probably the most important teaching period of the week. Here the coach comments on the performance of individuals, citing both good and bad play. It is of vital importance that he single out boys whose effort or technique is outstanding; however, most of his comments will be devoted to pointing out mental and physical errors and making suggestions for improvement. He does this by running a play over again on the screen as many times as is necessary to hammer home a point.

Clearly this is highly effective teaching. But it doesn't just happen. To prepare for this squad meeting the coaching staff must spend hours previewing the film. Only then can they make meaningful comments on each play when the boys are assembled.

But football is much more than the intellectual challenge I have sketched here. It offers a physical and emotional challenge as well. It is this combination that makes football such a great game.

The coach faces many problems that do not arise in the academic classroom. He is always dealing with a team. Players must work together to be successful in any phase of the game. If an individual does not execute his assignment, the offensive or defensive maneuver fails. And the individual player is accountable to his teammates as well as the coach for going offsides or for missing a block.

Emotion plays a large part in football. If the whole team pulls together well enough, they feel they did it together. The coach must instill in the team that desire to work together. He must also get through to individuals and build their self-confidence as parts of the whole.

Experienced coaches know they cannot do it alone. Success depends on the morale and unity of the group, led by individual players. If you do not have good student leadership, it is hard to be successful.

The coach must work to develop leaders, but sometimes key players are influenced negatively by parents and others who give them advice and instruction based on insufficient knowledge of the team or the game of football. Parents tend to be unhappy when their sons don't get enough playing time, and fans can be difficult after a loss.

The coach has many considerations that do not arise with an academic teacher. He must try to play everyone. This is often difficult or impossible, but the coach must do his best. It means a great deal to subs to participate. The coach should make sure to praise unsung players when they play well. Everyone notices the star running back, but few recognize the contributions of offensive linemen. The coach should not run up a score when he is lucky enough to be well ahead. That is not what sports are all about.

As a teacher of men, the coach should insist his players play hard, follow the rules, and display class. That means no taunting, profanity, or hot-dogging. The coach must set an example in his conduct and demeanor. Anyone will react by yelling at an incorrect call by an official, but a coach should not constantly criticize officials during a game. Over the years I have come in contact with some incompetent officials, but none who were biased or dishonest. If a coach has reason to doubt an official's competence, he should not carry on loudly throughout the game but go to the supervisor of officials later on.

No coach can get a bad call changed. And when he thinks about it, a coach knows unfavorable and favorable calls even out over time just like other breaks of the game.

Playing football is not easy. Physically it is one of the most demanding games we have. No boy should report for early practice unless he is in top physical condition. And once the workouts begin, he must continue to "pay the price" from the standpoint of effort expended all through the season. A wise coach, like any teacher, knows a little humor can lighten the daily grind and make for productive practices.

Somehow, in his teaching, a coach must sell his players on the necessity for consistency of performance. Obviously this means concentrating as hard as possible to eliminate mental errors. But it also means everybody going at top speed on every single play, regardless of fatigue or bruises. This is where motivation comes in.

There is strong evidence that football contributes more to the personal development of the students who participate than any academic subject. What classroom subject better teaches the values of perseverance, cooperation, and thorough preparation?

There is also good reason for believing that football coaches are among the best teachers to be found in American education today. Who is better prepared than the competent coach stepping onto the practice field? Who has put in longer hours deciding exactly what should be taught and how—and for exactly how many minutes? Who knows his students better? Who better motivates them to learn?

Who has a more accurate record of recent student performance than a football coach who thoroughly analyzes the film of Saturday's game? Who can demonstrate more clearly the value of correct techniques and extra effort than a coach who points out in the film the blocking that made possible a long run?

Surely football deserves a firm place in our educational thinking. And surely a good football coach is a good teacher.

DIAGRAMS and PHOTOGRAPHS Quick Reference

Index